"This book both educates and encourages. It educates by reminding us of the biblical facts of creation and the false teachings of evolution. It encourages the reader to know there is hope for positive change when we take our responsibilities seriously when voting or otherwise. It can be a terrific resource for any person who wants to be fully prepared to answer questions about creation and/or evolution and, most importantly, it clearly explains the need for each individual to know and accept Christ as Savior."
Ruth Haga, Locust Grove, VA

"Kevin, after reading your introduction, I feel you are on the right track in calling out those who think they have the right to determine what should fill our young people's heads. These are formative years of their young lives and should not be filled with 'theories' and not even given the chance to hear the 'REST OF THE STORY.' Go get them, Kevin."
Ralph H Gibson, Hanover, PA

"Kevin Turnbaugh presents a well-thought-out and logical defense for the presentation of Creationism, otherwise known as Intelligent Design, in schools. One of the purposes of science is to teach students to think outside the box and search for truth in ways that may not line up with prevailing thought. In order to do that, students should have all the information possible to make an informed, intelligent decision on any subject matter. There have been too many scientific 'discoveries' pointing to the truth of creation to discount it and remove it from the curriculum. By removing the study of Intelligent Design, schools are, in fact, not giving students the necessary facts needed to make an informed decision. This book should spark discussion and action on keeping or reinstating the teaching of Intelligent Design in the school system."
Kelly Grecco, Mason-Dixon Youth For Christ
Hanover, PA

Creation Is a Science

Why the Biblical Narrative Makes Sense

Kevin Turnbaugh

River Birch Press

Daphne, Alabama

Creation Is a Science: Why the Biblical Narrative Makes Sense
by Kevin Turnbaugh
Copyright ©2020 Kevin Turnbaugh
All rights reserved. This book is protected under the copyright laws of the United States of America. This book may not be copied or reprinted for commercial gain or profit.

Unless otherwise identified, Scripture is taken from the New King James Version (NKJV) of the Bible, unless otherwise noted, and were obtained through the on-line Bible Concordance known as Bible Gateway (www.biblegatgeway.com); and have been reviewed and applied in support of the issue addressed, and have been applied in context, to uphold the information provided in the pages of this book. References from any other publications will be noted at time of presentation.

ISBN 978-1-951561-10-9
For Worldwide Distribution
Printed in the U.S.A.

River Birch Press
P.O. Box 868
Daphne, AL 36526

*To the parents and students
who, despite their best efforts, are being
denied the teaching of Creation
(today known as Intelligent Design)
in their public schools*

Acknowledgments

Confrontational Christianity by Kevin Turnbaugh, Chapter 2, titled "The Myth of the Separation of Church and State" addresses the numerous court actions in the past that ruled that Christian symbols like crosses, Ten Commandments plaques or monuments, Christian flags, and anything associated with Christmas must be removed from public view, based on the mythical "Constitutional Separation of Church and State." The SCOTUS decision replaced the teaching of "Creation with Evolution" in the State of Louisiana which, based on the author's research, has never been reversed.

The Supreme Court of the United States (SCOTUS) case, Edwards v. Aguillard, June 19, 1987.

The Federal court case Kitzmiller v. Dover Area School District, December 20, 2005.

Contents

Introduction *ix*

1 Big Bang? *1*

2 From Creation to Noah *6*

3 Prehistoric Dinosaurs? *14*

4 Single Cell Beginning *20*

5 Bark, Meow, and Moo *25*

6 Botanical Life *30*

7 Same but Different *35*

8 Opposing Force *42*

9 "In God Is Our Trust" *46*

10 God's Control *50*

11 God's Will *54*

12 PTO Meetings *65*

13 The Church in Education *70*

14 Taking Down Evolution *76*

15 Creation A to Z *81*

16 Teaching the Truth *85*

Conclusion: No Is Unacceptable *88*

A Final Thought *93*

References *97*

Introduction

After the presidential election of 2004, when President George W. Bush was re-elected over his Democratic challenger Senator John Kerry, D-MA, many of the liberal television and radio commentators complained openly about how the large turnout of evangelical Christians kept Senator Kerry from the office he deserved. (The result of the 2016 election was also credited to the large turnout by those called evangelicals.)

This response was very noteworthy because it proved how the will of the people can and will put into office the person we desire to lead our nation and serve in that particular office. This right of the citizens of the United States of America, protected by the Constitution, applies to the state and local elected offices as well.

When the people of the USA do not take this right seriously, our nation will end up with less than desirable leaders, as was evident with the election and re-election of President Obama in 2008 and 2012.

Not casting a vote denies ourselves the right of expressing our feelings and desires at the voting booth. It will also affect how our nation, state, and even our local decisions are made and enforced. The old and totally invalid statement that my one vote cannot and will not make a difference is so very wrong. It is your one vote, combined with others of like-minded feelings, that will elect those who you wish to lead and make our laws, regulations, and ordinances that we must abide by in the future.

Among those actions and claims today that prevent people from voting are others trying to influence a vote result through threats at voting centers like those recently documented in Philadelphia by modern Black Panther members. When people or organizations try to stuff the ballot boxes, they enable a false and detrimental vote result, to the benefit of the candidate they wish to have elected to a particular office.

The backlash to a recent movement requiring voters to show proof of citizenship with a photo identification is another attempt to skew the voting results. This idea is being met with totally unsubstantiated claims that it prevents the elderly, the handicapped, and minorities from voting. Instead, the truth behind this claim is actually that this requirement prevents both ballot box stuffing and a vote by those without United States citizenship. I can personally attest to this, as I am blind; yet, I have several forms of photo identification. The federally mandated "Real ID Act" effective in May 2008, to be utilized by USA citizens to fly and also to enter federal buildings, should (in my opinion) be used as official identification to vote.

This fundamental right to vote should be used by the citizens of the USA to remove the incumbents if they do not agree with their actions. In addition, when initiatives or proposals are put forth to the people, the voting booth results give the currently serving elected officials a clear understanding of how the citizens of a state or local area wish for laws to be enacted.

We in the USA, and many other countries around the world, have this right to decide who will represent us in our government offices; however, this right is not available to the people of many other countries in the world. Some countries have a monarchy, where the rule of the King, Queen, Emperor, etc., decides what is best for the people. This type of rule usually benefits the sitting ruler and may even expand his or her control over the people.

Countries with dictatorial type leaders are ruled firmly and with iron fists, often adding to the hardships of the people. Other countries are ruled by those who base their leadership on religious beliefs, instilling upon the people fear that failure to follow them will result in adverse actions from their false and nonexistent gods.

When citizens, who do have the right and freedom to decide who does and does not serve as a representative of the people, do not exercise this right, the results can, and have in the past, resulted in rulings, laws, and just plain denial of those things the people desire. If not enough of the citizenry turns out to influence the results of a vote, nothing will change.

This is exactly what happened to the citizens who live in, and vote for those who serve on the school board of a local school district near my home a few years ago. The results of that election put in place board members who opposed the teaching of creation, which many today refer to as Intelligent Design.

Just a short time after these duly elected officials were sworn into their positions on the school board, they passed a resolution that directed the teaching of evolution only in the district and banned the teaching of creation entirely (based on the Federal Court ruling in Kitzmiller v. Dover Area School District, December 20, 2005).

Many of the parents, and even one sixteen-year-old girl featured in an interview on a local television station, expressed their great displeasure and demanded the school board change this ruling. However, the board chose not to appeal the decision to the Federal Court.

I have pounded the drums about threats on all things Christian in many of my past books, and this threat still exists today. The actions of the Federal Court Judge and this school board are just two examples of what steps opponents use to remove our God from our society. It is why voters who desire things like the teaching of Intelligent Design must make sure that they get to the voting booth and make their desires known.

Whether the official is a plain atheist, an agnostic, or just marches to his or her own drummer, it is quite apparent that they do not give a good rip if God is properly represented in our schools or not. Parents, students, and their local churches need to raise the roof about it in school board meetings. Let these officials know clearly that their decisions and actions are not the will of the people and that it will be made clear at the next election cycle.

When one takes the attitude that they cannot change things and what is happening is just God's will, then this kind of result will be realized more and more in our nation. We must, for the sake of our children attending our public schools, take a stand for God at meetings and especially at the voting booth. If your pastor tells you that voting is not for Christians, demand scripture to back up the statement. He or she will not find it because it does not exist. Instead, we need to get out there and make a difference through our votes. Elected officials have only one concern when re-election time comes and that is to be re-elected.

I have heard both sides of the argument on requiring term limits of officials in an office, and I must admit I lean toward being in favor of it. However, when there is someone in office who is doing good for the people and honoring God, people who hold this argument may be plunged into a great deal of confusion as to how to proceed in this matter.

After a long period of consideration, I decided to address the background of the issue on the teaching of evolution versus creation. What were the students in this school district being taught and what were they denied being taught by the federal court ruling and this school board? Just what do scientists and so-called experts try to force into the heads of our young people? Why do they feel that a theory, and a bad one at that, is so much more needed in our schools? Why are they opposed to the facts of creation and the world that God created? I will endeavor to answer many of these questions, what the theory has to offer and the facts that the Bible provides us.

You may be dealing with this issue, or maybe a totally unrelated but just as detrimental issue, in your area. In today's society, attacks on all things Christian are not just being felt, they are being imposed upon us, and our elected officials are keeping us from serving our God. We cannot just sit back and take a position of oh well, whatever God's will is that is the way it will be. Just as Jesus dealt with the money changers in the Temple, described in the Gospel books of Matthew, Mark, and John, we Christians must also make a difference and glorify God in doing so.

1

Big Bang?

When it comes to understanding how our universe, and all things here on earth, were created and came into existence, you will probably find as many opinions as you will find grains of sand on the shoreline. If you take ten scientists who claim to be experts and knowledgeable in how all things came into existence and interview each one separately, you will get ten different opinions about just what is meant by the "big bang" theory.

When it comes to what is commonly referred to as the Big Bang (first attributed to Edwin Hubble as part of Hubble's Law, and coined by Sir Fred Hoyle in 1949), I feel this theory has more holes in it than a slice of Swiss cheese. The information scientists give in order to support this theory is just as thin. The truth of the matter is that none of these so-called experts have even a clue. But it is also true that they cannot accept in any manner that God simply said the word, and all that we know to exist today came into existence.

I have found it very questionable when a so-called expert in a field has no historical data to support his or her opinion. Of course, they look at their opinion as fact, based on their detailed study of all things that exist. Before I let anyone tell me how the universe began, I want to know if they or someone in the past was there to document the point when they claim it all occurred.

Unlike the historians of old, such as the biblical historians named Josephus and Luke (who recorded his observations in the Gospel of Luke and in the book of Acts) and were present when events occurred that they have written about, the scientists and experts who hold to this theory of how our universe came into being are just plain guessing.

I am amused, yet saddened, when I learn of what new and wonderful discoveries the National Aeronautics and Space Administration (NASA) satellite research center, called the Jet Propulsion Laboratory (JPL), claim to be unique facts about our solar system and universe. Recently, the folks at JPL claim to have found an underground ocean on one of the moons of Jupiter. My first reaction was wondering if someone really went there and drilled down to find this ocean. Further in the article, it was made clear that this discovery was based solely on photos taken by the Hubble Space Telescope (HST) of that moon's surface.

I can only shake my head in disbelief that people who have thousands of hours of college training and spend countless hours staring out into space cannot see and fully understand that what is out there did not just happen as the result of a huge explosion.

The Bible makes it clear in the very first verse of Genesis that God created the heavens for His glory and according to His sovereign will. It also makes it clear that the earth was created to be the place where He would create man, and later woman, as well as the animals, plants, fish of the sea, and birds of the air (Genesis 1:1). Notice that the word "heavens" is plural, and "earth" is singular. Because of this, many biblical theologians believe and hold to the fact that life exists only on earth.

What is the theory behind the Big Bang? As I stated earlier in this chapter, you can probably find several opinions about how it is theorized to have happened. But there are two main

Big Bang?

ideas of thought on this ungodly theory. Both of them leave one wide open gap that must be answered for either of them to be even considered as fact, and that is where did the heavenly item come from, how was it made, and what brought it to the point that the Big Bang occurred?

The first theory we will look at is that of a single star. According to this line of thought, this star became very dense and eventually exploded into a supernova. According to information from NASA, a star will go supernova when its internal core becomes so dense that it cannot maintain its own gravity. When the star gets to this point, it will explode and, in time, form a black hole.

The scientists who hold to this theory of how the universe was formed have not explained where the star came from, and how this explosion created the world as we know it today without the resulting black hole. The information provided by NASA states that even light cannot escape a black hole. Based on this information, then how did all of the stars we see at night get distributed over what scientists claim to be billions of light years in distance? Although theorized that a massive black hole exists at the center of our galaxy, called the Milky Way, this has never been proven.

The other main theory claims that two heavenly bodies collided, and the resulting explosion formed the universe that we have today. Again, the question of where did these heavenly bodies come from needs to be answered. In the recent past, the HST caught the image of two stars colliding in space; however, this image was not anything like the one theorized by scientists in how our universe was formed.

At this point, scientists would argue about how Moses, who lived many centuries after the biblical creation described in Genesis chapters 1 through 3, and even after the biblical flood of Noah described in Genesis chapters 6 through 9; could have recorded the creation as a historical fact.

True, Moses, who wrote the books of Genesis, Exodus, Leviticus, Numbers, and Deuteronomy (also known by Jews as the Torah), wrote Genesis long after creation occurred. However, all of the authors of the books in the Bible wrote them by inspiration from God. In other words, God told them what to write, and in obedience to Him, recorded what we today know to be the Bible.

The reason scientists cannot just accept creation comes from the fact that to accept creation, one must then acknowledge that God exists, He is the sovereign ruler of the entire universe, and everything recorded in the Bible is true and factual. The problem scientists have is that they do not believe it can be as simple as God commanding something into existence, and it happens. No, they believe there must be a precise, analytical reason, explanation, or alternative way that the universe was formed.

Soon after I first started my job with the U.S. Army in 1987, a decision had to be made on how a particular issue would be handled requiring a mathematical result. A couple of engineers came in, took down the details and measurements, and said it would be about two weeks before they could provide an answer.

However, as a past industrial engineer myself, I looked at the proposal, did a couple of simple inputs in my calculator, and had the answer in five minutes. They laughed at me and went off to their detailed analysis. When they returned two weeks later, they had the answer, and it just so happened to be the same thing I had come up with in only five minutes.

The point of this story is that some people just cannot accept that God simply created the heavens and the earth in a

Big Bang?

matter of six actual days. The same can be said to those who cannot accept that God, His Son Jesus Christ, requires only a simple prayer of requesting forgiveness for sins and accepting Jesus as our Savior to guarantee our future in heaven. Instead, they believe there must be an enormous amount of number crunching, and a narrow-minded view of how things came into existence, and it just cannot involve a supreme being like God.

The fact is that evolution's theory of how all was created via the Big Bang is plainly unable to be proven. Where did the star or stars come from, what caused the explosion, and how did this occurrence put all the galaxies, stars, nebulas, comets, planets, and the sun into the perfect position they are, without design from God? My questions in this chapter alone have placed scientists into a black hole they cannot reason their way out of, because they cannot even defend what they stand for or even agree on how the universe came into existence.

As we proceed through the pages of this book, we will deal with many other aspects of what evolution tries to teach us, and how these claims cannot be supported or substantiated. We will use facts from Biology and Botany, along with many other science-based facts, to show how this theory is just that and a bad one too.

I would challenge you, the reader, to understand that God never intended things to be so complex, that to fully understand and believe what is in the Bible is true will require some kind of advanced analysis. Instead, He created all we know to exist as described in Genesis.

2

From Creation to Noah

Read Genesis chapters 1 through 9 and Revelation 12:7-10.

When you begin reading Genesis 1, you will see in verse 1 that "God created the heavens and the earth." Then in verse 2, we read, "and the earth was without form and void." Many of you may be thinking that if God is so perfect, why did He create the earth as described in verse 2? Unfortunately, the answer is not very clear, and theologians debate it to this day.

In the reading I listed for this chapter above, I have included a portion of scripture from the last book of the Bible, in Revelation 12. Although it is unknown and not fully explained in the Bible, some theologians believe that between verses 1 and 2 of Genesis 1, the fall of Satan and the angels of heaven who followed him may have occurred and caused all that God had created to become less than perfect. Because of this, God then began the six days of creating what we know to exist today and then rested on the seventh day.

I will not, nor can anyone else, say that this is precisely what caused the earth to be "without form and void." This is just the first item or situation described in the Bible that has no explanation or can be proven. As Christians, we believe that many of those things we cannot understand here on earth will be explained to us in heaven, and this is part of believing in God by faith.

It is this faith that helps us to believe that what Moses recorded in the book of Genesis, even though they all occurred before his birth, is true and historically correct. God told Moses what to write down, and the result of that writing is what we call the book of Genesis.

As you read through the verses in chapters 1 through 5, we see where God created day and night, the land and the seas, the plants, animals, birds of the air, and the fish in the sea. Finally, God created man in His own image from the dust of the earth He had just commanded into existence.

This first man, named Adam, was then commanded by God to give names to all the animals He had created before Adam's creation. After a period of time, God created a woman using one of Adam's ribs, and Adam named her Eve (Genesis 2:21-23; 3:20).

After this point in Genesis, just a few chapters cover many thousands of years. Adam and Eve are parents to Cain and Abel along with many other sons and daughters, including Seth (Genesis 5:3); from these descendants, the entire earth was populated. During this time, people experienced longevity of life as Adam lived nine hundred thirty years (Genesis 5:5), and many of his descendants lived very long lives as well as listed in the same chapter.

Here is another point in the Bible where debates occur about how long the earth and the universe have existed. Theologians have used the time frames described in Genesis 5, then added the years since the flood occurred to come up with a reasonable estimate of how long all things have existed from God's creation to today. But so many ifs, what-abouts, and how-do- you-explains are part of this debate. In the following chapters, we will look at detailed arguments, theories, and claims from the evolution theory and the facts from creation. But at this point, we are going to look at the evidence of world population before the flood.

The first piece of evidence we are going to look at is the only one my research found to be above sea level today. In the far eastern end of the modern-day country of Turkey, known in Bible New Testament times as Asia Minor, will be found one of the higher mountain ranges on earth, the Ararat mountain range and specifically Mount Ararat itself. It is here that we will find the most compelling evidence of the flood and the voyage of Noah and his family in the Ark built according to God's instructions by Noah and the workers before the flood (Genesis 6:14-15).

On a plateau, on the left side of the mountain, rests the Ark itself. I can make this claim because the Bible says so (Genesis 8:4) and because several expeditions since the late 1800s have traveled to the area of Mount Ararat actually have seen the Ark. In addition, people living in that part of Turkey have also seen and described the Ark on Mount Ararat.

Finally, there exists photographic evidence taken by U2 spy aircraft during the very late 1950s into the early 1960s. They flew over this area on their way to the Union of Soviet Socialist Republics (USSR) to photograph the missile sights set up by the Soviets that were pointed at Europe.

I have a DVD recording I ordered from the store associated with the History Channel (now just called History) of their documentary on the voyage of Noah. Among the evidence they present is a stone engraved with a notation about the epic of a man called Gilgamesh, which the History DVD claims can be translated Noah.

It is in this documentary that they interview a former CIA employee, who had personally looked at and studied the photos taken by the U2 aircraft, showing the Ark in detail. Although

From Creation to Noah

the photos are still classified as of the writing of this book, the evidence is there in the archives of the CIA.

Another piece of evidence comes from the government of Turkey itself, as they have stated that there is a boat-like structure found on Mount Ararat. Today, the Ark is completely covered by a glacier on the mountain, but the evidence of Noah's Ark is plentiful and very hard to deny.

Another piece of evidence provided by our friends at History came in another documentary about the underwater pyramids of Japan. In this DVD, we are shown the underwater images of pyramids, much like those found in the jungles of southern Mexico and other Central American countries, as well as arch-like structures and even paved roads. These items are also found in the Sea of Japan in as shallow of water as only sixty feet and as deep as four hundred feet.

In this same documentary, evidence is shown of an entire city off the shores of India completely submerged, with all of the homes and other structures intact. Also, we can see a line of very large stone structures lying on the Atlantic Ocean floor, just off from the Bahamas, that archeologists have called the Bimini Road. These stone structures that look like a fallen wall on the ocean floor, and the recently found buildings submerged in the Gulf of Mexico, have given rise to what some claim to be possibly the remains of the long lost continent of Atlantis.

It is so interesting, if not compelling, how similar the Mayan pyramids of Mexico and Central America are to the underwater pyramids found off the shore of Japan. Those interviewed in this documentary estimate the underwater pyramids to be about nine thousand years old, very close to the estimate theologians have estimated the earth and the universe to be since God created all things. Yet, these same so-called experts say these underwater structures are merely the result of the last ice age and give no credence to the flood.

Two other pieces of evidence I feel prove that the world was completely populated before the flood; however, no one in the science world or even most theologians relate them to their origins and how they arrived at their location, or how they even exist. These pieces of evidence also exist above sea level. The first one is located in England, and the second on the most isolated landmass on earth called Easter Island in the Pacific Ocean, which is now claimed by the country of Chile.

In the English countryside, an unexplained, yet often theorized about stone structure known as Stonehenge can be found. Many feel this structure is an oversized sundial that determines the date or time of year based upon when the sun appears through the stones in a certain position and manner. Also, many believe that Stonehenge was constructed to be a religious place, and some have given credit to the Druids as the builders. However, nobody really knows who built it, when it was built, or even how it was built as the stones that make up this structure are estimated to weigh many tons.

Nowhere on earth, even underwater, has another structure like it been found whether in any state of ruin or intact. Why was it built just in England, and why in that particular location? Some of the stones look like they had fallen off from where they had been originally placed on top of other vertical stones, yet they still remain in a circular position that just happens to allow the light from the sun to come through the stones at a specific day and time of year.

One other piece of evidence lacking about Stonehenge is that neither the peoples of ancient Scotland, like those depicted in the movie "Braveheart," nor the peoples of that same time period from England and Wales have recorded in their history any mention of this stone structure's existence.

From Creation to Noah

Finally, located over two thousand miles from the closest landmass, making it the most isolated place on earth, is found the tiny island in the middle of the Pacific Ocean called Easter Island. This island, now part of the nation of Chile, is populated by less than six thousand people, of which only about half are natives called Rapa Nui, as well as seagulls and other types of birds. It is visited by tourists and scientists several times a year.

People come to see, wonder, and theorize about the numerous and enormous sized stone-carved heads found all over the island. These huge heads stand as silent guardians of the island, and although not exactly all alike, they are very similar in appearance and size.

Known as Moai by the native islanders, scientists claim that they were carved sometime between the twelfth and sixteenth centuries, and represent those who had passed on from life. This island and its giant carved image were not discovered until early in the eighteenth century; however, except for what is claimed by the islanders, how these images exist is still a matter of debate. Thought to weigh many tons each, how they were moved and placed is not an established fact.

In the biblical story of Noah, the building of the Ark, and the subsequent flood, found in Genesis 6 through 9, Noah was instructed to build the Ark. God told him that He was going to destroy the earth's inhabitants because of the people's evil. Only Noah and his family were found to be honoring God, so they were the only ones that would survive the devastation that God would cause. The people He had created had gone away from God, were committing grievous sins, serving other gods (maybe like the heads on Easter Island), and God had had enough.

So Noah received from God the Ark's dimensions and how it would be built, even down to the type of wood to be used (Genesis 6:14-15). At the ripe old age of six hundred years,

Creation Is a Science

Noah began building of the Ark, which was to be approximately four hundred-fifty feet long, seventy-five feet wide, and forty-five feet high.

Up until this time, the earth had not been refreshed by rain, but instead, God had created it in such a way that it was watered by a mist that rose from under the ground (Genesis 2:6). Hearing Noah's claim that the world would be destroyed by a flood, one could imagine how the people made fun of Noah, although others probably helped him build the Ark.

Then at the given time, God caused the animals of the earth to come to the Ark in pairs (one male and one female) to preserve their kind, and Noah and his family entered the Ark, and God closed the door. The rain came and lasted for forty days and nights until the earth was entirely submerged underwater, and the Ark floated above the floodwaters for one hundred-fifty days before landing on the plateau of Mount Ararat.

Once the land was dry enough for Noah, his sons, their families, and all the animals to disembark from the Ark, Noah built an altar and worshipped God, thanking Him for saving them from the destruction of the earth.

God then made a covenant between Noah and Himself, that He would never judge the earth in this same manner again. God created the rainbow that is seen by all to this day, as a permanent sign of this covenant with Noah.

It is shameful, and I am personally offended, that today this same symbol has been adopted by the lesbian, gay, bisexual, and transgender (LGBTQ) community, as a sign of their right to live their sinful lifestyle. It's just another indication how man and woman have turned away from God in today's world, similar to how the people of Noah's time had also turned away from God.

All of us need to examine our lives and make sure we do not

have something we put before our worship of God. In everything we say and do, at our jobs, in our families, and in our social areas of life, we need to keep God in the center in obedience to the First Commandment.

3

Prehistoric Dinosaurs?

If you ever take a trip to Washington D.C., a must-see are the several buildings that surround The Mall and are operated by the Smithsonian Institute. You can visit a sculpture museum, the castle which is the original Smithsonian museum, the American History museum, and the most visited museum on the National Mall called the Air and Space Museum.

Located in the middle of the National Mall can be found the Smithsonian's Museum of Natural History. Just about anything from nature can be seen inside this Museum, including a working beehive, insects of all sizes (some dead and some very much alive). In the precious stones area, rare stones, like the Hope Diamond, unusual crystal formations, etc. can be viewed. Then we come to the area of the museum where you will find the reconstructed bone structures of extinct dinosaurs.

Look up to the ceiling, and you will see the bones of a pterodactyl, which was a flying dinosaur with one mean set of teeth in its head. Greeting you as you enter the room is old T-Rex himself or herself (as the case may be), a fully reconstructed Tyrannosaurus Rex. During my last visit, which I must admit was quite some time ago when I still had my sight, a three-horned tank of a dinosaur called a triceratops was reconstructed behind the old T-Rex.

The skeleton of Cro-Magnon Man is standing over in one corner of this first room. I find it very hard to deny that di-

Prehistoric Dinosaurs?

nosaurs existed when I am looking directly at their bones; however, when it comes to a caveman in another corner, it was not hard for me to know that one was a phony.

I pegged what that skeleton was in a New York minute—that of a gorilla standing straight up. I welcome you to check me out. Go see our caveman friend at the museum, take along a photo of a forest gorilla from Africa, and tell me that the foreheads are not the same. The facial structure is so similar that it is silly—the look is so much the same. The dinosaur bones are real, but the caveman is another story altogether.

What I cannot tell you in this book is anything about when these creatures walked the earth, and how they became extinct. The Bible does mention something about giants existing in the land (Genesis 6:1-4); however, many researchers of this part of the Bible think this is referencing a very large people believed to have descended from mating between some of Satan's fallen angels and women who were daughters of Adam and Eve, and subsequent pairings of their children and grandchildren, named the Nephilim.

On this subject, the most hotly debated issue is how long ago these creatures lived. Many paleontologists are convinced that dinosaurs lived millions of years ago, but their evidence is based on the highly contested accuracy of Carbon 14 testing. They claim that their bones were preserved by fossilization, which is a hardening of the bones to almost a stone density. They say this is the reason they did not deteriorate over the centuries into dust.

But, here again we run into differences of opinions and theories of how they became extinct and how we have their fossilized bones today. Although we do have the bones, I find myself doubting here. Why were only the dinosaurs fossilized, but you do not hear much about this type of preservation today!

These differing theories are so many; you could put them on a wheel, spin it, and choose which one is the next opinion or theory to be used. From freezing to death in an ice age, to a comet hitting the earth and incinerating them, to what we call today climate change or global warming—all of these theories have their problems with being proven. What really is the reason these creatures died off where none of them exist in any form today if they truly existed at all? It would be simple for me just to say God only knows, but that just might be the only source for this answer, and I will have to wait until I am called home to heaven to find out.

One idea of how they died off was that they were not preserved by God at the time of the flood, but even I would argue that an explanation would be needed for those known to have existed in the water. Such dinosaur age water creatures like a trilobite, or some other type of creature may have lived in the seas at that time. However, I am not dismissing God's intervention and His decision to simply remove these creatures from His creation.

One would wonder if any still exist. A few years ago off the shores of the African island nation of Madagascar, a sports fisherman caught a fish, long thought to be extinct from the age of dinosaurs, called a coelacanth. In fact, in my research for this area of the book, I found a website that lists ten different fish that exist today, which are believed to be from the age of dinosaurs, including the fish we get caviar from called a sturgeon.

According to many wildlife researchers, naturalists, zoologists, and others involved in the study of animals, we are experiencing the extinction of animals every day. In the most recent history of the USA alone, we came very close to bringing the buffalo and gray wolf to extinction, and the gray wolf is still in danger of this occurring if the trapping of these beautiful ani-

Prehistoric Dinosaurs?

mals is not stopped soon.

In the past, the dodo bird of islands near Madagascar in the Indian Ocean became extinct, and the hunting of the rare white tiger for its fur is threatening another creation of God. But the most famous threat to extinction in our more modern times was the wholesale hunting of the whales for their blubber from which oil was extracted and used for many purposes worldwide.

One of the most significant efforts to save and preserve a creation of God was the protection of the bald eagle. Today, this resilient bird and symbol of the USA has made a remarkable comeback, and mating couples can be seen in many parts of the country.

However, this brings us back to why the dinosaurs became extinct. We cannot deny they existed, or can we? They are not documented in the pages of the Bible, but there is just too much factual evidence to the earth only being about ten to fifteen thousand years old and not nearly a billion as some scientists would have you believe.

Nor can we give any credit to the claim of dinosaurs, and man for that fact, living as long ago as millions of years ago. Some Bible researchers connect the descriptive references of the "behemoth" in Job 40:15, and the "leviathan" in Job 41:1, as dinosaurs; however, the footnotes provided for these verses in the NKJV state that they are unknown land or sea creatures.

I put the knowledge of all things dinosaur into the same category as the theory of the Big Bang and how the universe was formed. Nobody was there; they existed before history was recorded, and/or God chose to not record their existence within the pages of the Bible.

The purpose of the Bible is to document the history of man from Adam and Eve and record things from history that we can learn from and prevent from happening again. Most importantly, the Bible was written so we can learn about God and how all things came to a point where His Son, Jesus Christ, came to earth and died on a cruel Roman cross to pay the ultimate price for our sins.

We cannot deny what we see, as the bones of the dinosaurs are right in front of us. The remains of dinosaur age animals can be seen in other places like Los Angeles' La Brea Tar Pits, etc. However, outside of these bones and remains, there is no independent evidence of these creatures. One fact that weighs heavy with me comes from the lack of any mention of these kinds of giants in the Bible (the exception would be the Job references above). All references, like what I provided earlier, are of humans. When we do read of animals in the Bible, they all refer to animals we see today, like camels, donkeys, and sheep.

In the beginning chapters of Genesis, we read of the serpent approaching Eve and speaking to her about eating from the forbidden tree in the middle of the garden. This creation of God had been indwelled by Satan (Genesis 3:1-5), and after he tempted Eve, both Adam and Eve sinned against God. Among the names given to Satan is the "great deceiver." Deception comes in many forms, and Satan has used all of them many times to sway people away from God and condemn them to hell for eternity.

It might surprise you to learn that I believe in the existence of Unidentified Flying Objects (UFOs) and that people have actually seen them. But here is where that great deceiver moniker that Satan wears comes into play. I do not dismiss the idea that Satan creates those visual sightings to cause people to believe in life out in space and move them away from God. I believe it is possible that Satan could have done the same deception with the bones we are finding here on earth that we call dinosaurs.

Prehistoric Dinosaurs?

If you read the book of Job in the Bible, you will learn that Satan is not powerless, as he was allowed by God to test Job's faith up to a point, but that he could not kill him. Satan killed all of Job's children, removed his animals from him, and caused boils to form on Job from head to toe. Job was unshaken, and God eventually restored him. However, this story shows that Satan can and does use all manner of ways to deceive one from believing in God, and nobody should ever sell Satan short of what he can and will do to cause people to turn from God.

A question that you may have is why God allows Satan to do these things. Welcome to the club, because so many times I have asked the same thing. It is so simple just to say God is sovereign, and that He is in control of all things; however, it can be difficult to understand the whys and reasonings for God allowing things to occur. I wish God would answer that question once in a while, but some things will not be understood until we see Him face to face in heaven, and this is where faith in God and His control of all things come in to play in a Christian's life.

Reader, the most important issue you need to be concerned about is whether Jesus Christ is your Savior. Do you remember a day when you asked Him into your heart, to forgive you of your sins, and accept Him as the Lord of your life? If not, I would refer you to the book of John in the Bible and chapter 3. There you will learn how Jesus can become the Savior of your life, by your becoming born again in the spirit of God. If you make this decision, I encourage you to find a local Bible church, tell the pastor what you have done, and let them show you more from the Bible, and disciple you in your spiritual growth in the Lord. The dinosaurs may or may not have existed, but God is very real; and so is the decision you make to accept or reject Him. The difference is your eternal future in heaven or hell.

4
Single Cell Beginning

I am a student of history and have a desire to understand what others might think as trivial. In fact, I have been quite good at playing the game Trivial Pursuit, including the Bible trivia oriented game. Some time ago, I learned that a person cannot count from one to a trillion in their lifetime because nobody can live a trillion seconds. Even if you could start counting at birth, you would not get to a trillion before you died of old age.

Okay, so what does this have to do with the contents of this book? Not only can one not count to a trillion, but we also cannot conceive of exactly how many cells make up the human body. From what I could find out, nobody has even considered trying, since the body is made up of quad-trillions of cells. All of them are microscopic and include skin cells, both red and white blood cells, stem cells and brain cells, cells in our stomach that excrete acid that digests our food and drink for energy and health, and the list goes on.

If we are to believe those who insist that all things started with the Big Bang, the next thing that occurred was the basic chemicals that form life came together, and the first life form came into being as a single cell something. The best known single cell life form, outside of the human body is known as the amoeba, but it is not the only known single cell something. Anybody who has had a cold, influenza, or any other virus has

Single Cell Beginning

experienced what those little somethings can do to the human body.

Scientists would have us to believe that all life, as we know it today, came from this very something through evolution. Not even the best used car salesman in the world could sell this story to me as fact. As with the Big Bang, I need to know where these chemicals even came from, how they just happened to be on the piece of the star or stars that formed earth, and how they happened to be at the same place at the same time to complete the chemical reaction needed to form life. I don't know about you, but I could probably be talked into buying the Brooklyn Bridge before I would buy into this story.

Let's look at something we know more about, and that is our own human body. Biologists will tell you that our bodies are made up of several different chemicals, and the main one is water, which is two parts hydrogen and one part oxygen (H_2O). In addition, the air we breathe is a combination of oxygen and nitrogen, and the foods we eat have multiple vitamins needed for a healthy body to function.

Somehow we are to believe that all the needed chemicals required to form life were at the same place, at just the right time, and in the perfect amounts to form this single cell life. The next thing we are told is that this something lived in the water. In time it evolved into small fish, then to larger aquatic creatures like salamanders, and eventually a creature that came out of the water onto dry land. From this point, something crawled on the ground, then onto all fours, then to just the two hind legs, until we finally have man.

Somewhere down this line of fiction, I lost how we evolved into both man and woman. We started out as a single cell something, but I do not see where it evolved into a two cell something, a one hundred cell something, etc. By the way, where did the water come from, where the single cell something started?

The next thing I need explained to me is if all life came from this same single cell something, how is it that today we have fish, salamanders, and both cold- and warm-blooded creatures, and humans? How did we humans evolve from the same single cell that produced scorpions, horses, armadillos, manatees, doves, reindeer, and squirrels? I must have missed the memo somewhere, but none of these creatures have a thing in common with humans. In addition, how did humans come from the same source that produced the insects that are all over the world in more varieties, colors, and functions than one could count on our fingers and toes together?

Here is where the rubber meets the road on this issue. We did not all come from a single cell something. In fact, none of the life forms found on earth came from anything but from the sovereign will of God. However, scientists just cannot allow themselves to accept that there is a God, a supreme being who is in control of all things large and small. Also, they cannot explain their evolutionary stand but insist that we must believe it as fact. The simple idea of God commanding all that we know on earth into existence just cannot be accepted by these so-called highly educated folks.

The medical world will tell you that the body is one of the most sophisticated and complex organisms known. Animals are just as complex in their own way; however, our concern is the human body. We are the products of our parents mating and the interaction of a female egg and a male sperm, both of which are microscopic themselves. Yet, from those two components, a human body is formed consisting of miles of arteries and veins, a superhighway system that makes up the nerves, muscles, skin, bones, and the numerous organs that are part of the body as a whole. The world's best computer is found inside of the cranial

Single Cell Beginning

cavity known as the brain, from which everything in the body operates.

In addition, from these two microscopic creations of God will come the best cameras ever made called the eyes, the audio receivers called the ears, and something unique to each person, our fingertips that contain a pattern that no other person has, including identical twins or triplets. Science is looking into using the retina of the eye to make even a more specialized identifier of each person.

I have viewed, with great amusement I must admit, the many shows and documentaries that try to show how we humans evolved from chimpanzees. Yet, the Natural History Museum has the skeleton of a gorilla as supposedly being early man. These so-called experts in man's evolution talk about how similar we are to chimps, but I have yet to see them produce even the remains of something between to verify their claim that we came from this type of animal. Where is the infamous missing link? To date, nobody has been able to capture a creature referred to as Bigfoot, or what the Native American Indians call Sasquatch, and I do not believe they ever will as I doubt the existence of such a creature.

Again, we return to an ongoing question in this book. Why do scientists insist that we must have come from a single cell something, formed after the baseless theory of the Big Bang? We return to the same answer as well, and that is their unbelief in God, that no supreme being is in control, and that things just cannot be as simple as God said it, and it was so.

Any scientist worth his or her college training does not like a broad area of possibilities because they want to zero in on the answer in a short time. Yet, in the case of evolution, there are so many ideas, theories, suggestions, and just plain wild guesses; how all things came to be. But, it is we Christians who are called narrow-minded, because we simply trust in God, and believe the biblical story of creation. My question to the scientists is why can't the answer be just that simple?

Since writing this chapter, my wife and I watched the new documentary series called Planet Earth 2 on BBC America. Many of God's creations were observed in their natural habitats, but one of these creatures was new to me. They showed an insect from the Amazon River area of South America called the railroad worm. It is a multi-legged creature that is luminous at night, and it is deadly poisonous. I would invite any subscriber to the idea of evolution to prove to me, and many others, how we humans evolved from the same individual source that also evolved into this deadly insect.

5

Bark, Meow, and Moo

Read Genesis 1:20-25.

In a recent newscast, I heard that Americans spend several billion dollars a year feeding pets and on supplies for their pets. Over three quarters of homes today have at least one pet that is part of the family. Currently, my wife and I have one dog (which is my guide dog), and some cats, or as we refer to it as a zoo. Each one of our pets have their own unique quirks, so each of them does things a little differently. The dog eats like the house is on fire. Then there are the cats that do things each in their own different ways and keep us guessing.

The same is true all around the world. There are as many different animals as there are square miles on earth (if you include the fish in the oceans and seas). Some are found everywhere, like dogs and cats, and others are indigenous to only a particular area. Some are unique to themselves, and others have several different species of the same animal.

Some have no fear of man and even interact with us, and others avoid man in any possible way. There are those who pose no threat to man, and there are those who are best left alone and avoided, as they can severely injure and even kill a man.

In the scripture reading I listed for this chapter, we are told that God created all the animals, birds, and fish in the waters. That is simple enough, but science would have us believe that all life evolved from the single cell we wrote about in the previous chapter. This only raises numerous questions that they just do not want to address. Of course, I would like God to explain why we needed to have hornets, venomous snakes, and deadly sea creatures like the deadliest creature on earth known as the box jellyfish; however, their creation was just as much a part of His sovereign will as that of dogs and cats.

Science just cannot explain why we have so many different types of animals as well as different species within each kind of animal. When we look at all the breeds of dogs registered with the American Kennel Club (AKC) alone, we who believe the Bible cannot explain these different animal species either. This would apply to the cats as well, when we consider they range from our household type cuddlers, up to the big cats like lions and tigers in the wild.

I do not want to bore you with all kinds of trivial facts, but as an expansion on my previous chapter, let's just consider how vast a difference of animals, fishes, and insects we have in the world and their associated species.

When was the last time you visited your local Society for the Prevention of Cruelty to Animals (SPCA) kennel and viewed all the different dogs and cats they have up for adoption? Being the animal lovers that my wife and I are, we try not to go too often because we would probably take them all if we had the room and land to hold and care for them. However, on any visit you will find big dogs like rottweilers and small dogs like terriers or those even smaller. The same goes for the cats on hand. From the multiple colored domestic short hair to unique breeds like a Siamese, they are all different kinds of cats.

Looking back to our friend Noah and the voyage of the Ark, and knowing that God caused the animals to come on board in pairs, one would have to wonder where they put all the different breeds and species of each on the Ark. Was it really that big to hold all of them? God designed the Ark, so it must have been perfectly prepared to hold all of Noah's family and that of his son's families along with the creatures from the earth that were to be spared the destruction of the flood.

Add to this the fact that Noah and his family members would have had to store food onboard for each of the animals as well. This alone would have been a mighty task when you consider giant pandas eat bamboo, koala bears eat eucalyptus tree leaves, and the big cats eat other animals, just as examples.

The point we need to understand here is that scientists would have us believe as fact that all things living on this earth came from that same single cell something. Now just consider how diverse all the living creatures are from each other. How in the name of common sense could we humans, with all of our facial and structural differences have come from the same source that produced the eight-legged spiders, all of the other different types of spiders, elephants, and the devils who live on the island of Tasmania? Some insects are very tiny like fleas and ticks, and others are large and not so friendly like the army ants that can outright kill a human, and still others are like the mighty painful hornets that come in different colors themselves.

I may be a little off my rocker, but I would just love to debate an evolutionist and lay into them with all of these facts. I want to hear them stumble over-explaining why some cattle have little or short horns, and others have long ones like the longhorn cattle best known from Texas. To top that, can they explain how we have cattle, buffaloes, yaks, oxen, and the water buffalo, all animals that live in different parts of the earth?

Why do we have little spiders like the household wolf spider, and we also have mean spirited ones like the black widow and the tarantula? Then I would bomb them with all of

Creation Is a Science

the different kinds of birds, fish, and the list would be endless.

You could expand the argument in so many ways. Why do we have birds that fly, and others who do not like the emu and penguins; why are some found everywhere and others only in certain parts of the world?

In some places on earth, you do not want to go for a little walk without some kind of protection with you. In the area of Southeast Asia, you could walk up upon a king cobra, or into the range of a komodo dragon, and wish you were somewhere else real quick. Some monkeys are small and totally harmless, and others could hurt you like a baboon or some type of gorilla. Do not walk under trees in South America, or a boa could just fall on you and squeeze you to death.

I believe I would have a pretty good chance of completely messing up the evolutionist and not even touch all of the animals, fish, insects, etc. known to man. It all comes back to their almost desperate desire to deny the existence of God and the fact that a supreme being is in control of the universe. In the next chapter, we will look at a totally different, yet similar type of life on earth, to see if they can explain their existence too.

What we do not know, nor can anyone explain, is that in God's almighty power and sovereign will, He created all the animals, insects, birds, etc. that we have on earth. Only God could have directed the animals onto the Ark, and upon their coming out caused them to multiply into the species and numbers we have today. God controls all things here on earth, and this includes the creatures from the mighty elephant to the microscopic mites.

Maybe you have realized that God does exist, and all we find in the Bible is true after all, including the ultimate sacrifice Jesus Christ made on that cross for your sins. Now is a good time for you to get on those knees, ask Him to forgive you of your sins, and accept Him as the Savior of your life. I sincerely hope you do, and if not here on earth, I desire to meet you in heaven.

6

Botanical Life

Read Genesis 1:11-13, 2:4-6.

Up to this point, we have looked at how evolutionists claim all things came into being, from the baseless Big Bang theory and the just as unsubstantiated single cell source of our existence. We have looked at what was before the flood, and what exists now since the flood. In addition, we have dealt with all things living on earth, or have we?

We humans and the creatures here on earth breathe in air for survival, and fish filter water through their gills for the same reason. Some biologists believe that some insects simply absorb what they need to survive.

However, we have not dealt with all living things yet. There is a totally different kind of life all over the earth that keeps us as humans, along with the animals, alive and helps us survive. I am talking about everything from the great Sequoias found in California to our little house plants like ferns and mini cactus. This would also include the grasses and even the kelp in the oceans.

These living creations are just as diverse as animals and have just as many species. According to the reading I provided for this chapter, they have been here longer than the animals and we humans. There is not a botanist alive that will not tell you that these plant creations are just as much alive as any animal.

Botanical Life

Sure, they do not have arteries and veins like humans, nor do they have the organs found in many different kinds of animals as well as us humans. Instead, they are living things that do many things like us, including reproduction of their own kind.

In this chapter, we are going to throw another wrinkle into the evolutionists claim that all life came from that single cell something. They claim that ALL (and I capitalized that word on purpose) life came from this same source. I am going to have a field day showing how baseless and totally untrue this stand by evolutionists really is and why. This is also an area they do not want to address because it does disprove their theory of evolution entirely.

The first thing we want to look at takes us back to the chemicals needed to create life. They seem to want us to believe that these things came together at just the right time and place for life to form. Their claim would have to show that the exact mix of hydrogen, oxygen, nitrogen, and many more chemicals like potassium and other vitamin-based minerals had to be there.

But we would also need something called carbon dioxide (CO_2) to be present. This chemical mixture is indeed poisonous to us and other animals too; however, take a guess what kind of living things absorb this mixture for their survival.

The fact is that God created the world we live in with many different types of plants and airborne chemicals and gases. I could list a chapter full of what we know to exist, like helium, radon, and on the list would go. We also have plants that are just as diverse, from the beautiful rose bush with its thorns to deadly plants like those that actually inject anthrax into the air. Some are as gentle as a pansy, and others can be unpleasant to the touch like poison ivy and oak. Here again, we could ask God why He created some of these types of plants, but the answer is the same—it was His sovereign will to do so.

Getting back to creation versus evolution, if the evolutionists are to be believed, then their Big Bang occurrence would have had to do more than form the planets, stars, comets, etc. This occurrence would have had to form the many gases needed for survival, and this would not have come from that single cell something for sure.

Denying that God exists and that He had nothing to do with what we know to be in our world today is without a basis of fact. Although other planets have a type of atmosphere on or around them, like that of Venus, our earth is the only known place that contains an atmosphere capable of sustaining life at all. This fact puts another nail into the theory of evolution, because how these particular gases came and formed on earth, and not Venus or Mars, would need to be explained, and they would not be able even to know where to start.

The plants of earth do not breathe in the carbon dioxide like we do the oxygen/nitrogen atmosphere. Instead, they absorb this chemical mixture, and combined with the water their roots draw up from the ground and catch by their leaves and branches, they obtain the life-sustaining nutrients they require to survive. Then the plants release the oxygen/nitrogen mixture we need to survive. This makes the plants a vital part of maintaining life on earth all around. Without them, we would run out of air to breathe, and so would the animals. You see, what the plants release from their life functions is the oxygen/nitrogen air we breathe, and what we exhale into the atmosphere is the CO_2 they need to absorb. One without the other and both cease to exist. This exchange of life-sustaining chemicals is also not lost in our oceans and rivers. In God's perfect creation of all things, He made it possible for this exchange to occur between the fishes and the plants that live on or under the surface of the water.

Botanical Life

The evolutionists stand on their so-called detailed analysis. They say we began as that single cell something, evolved in the waters, then came onto land, and through various steps eventually became what we know today to be men and women. Another fallacy in that theory is revealed here because I have never seen a tree walk or move. If everything came from that cell in the water, then how did the trees get to where they are?

I know grass can spread over a land area, and this is accomplished by their seeds being spread by the wind. The same would go for tree seeds, those pesky dandelion weeds in our yards included, but I cannot say I know of a plant that crawls or walks.

Another avenue on this discussion are those plants that provide food to the animals and to us humans. Many animals feed on the grasses found around the world, and even others like our cuddly friend, the koala bear in Australia, feed on the leaves of eucalyptus trees. Berries from many bushes in Africa are the source of food for some monkeys, and others feed off termites. Then you have those plants we feed off of ourselves like corn stocks, apple trees, and one of my favorites, the potato.

In the fall of the year, my thoughts go to pumpkin pie. But other plants produce those numerous vegetables and fruits you see in any produce area of a grocery store. From asparagus to zucchini, and everything in between, we can thank God for them, because they did not come from that single cell something.

The evolutionists, who try to cram their so-called evidence down our throats, and especially those of our school-aged children, just do not want you to think about these points. They would rather we just accept what they say and don't ask questions. My purpose in this book is to raise many questions for them, all of which debunk their precious theory that we came from some Big Bang to what we are today.

Creation Is a Science

For those of you who work on a computer, you have probably heard the saying about "garbage in, garbage out." The evolutionists are trying to do this to us as well. They are almost desperately trying to convince everybody, but especially our children in our schools, that this is how it happened. There is no supreme being who directed things into place like God, it was just something that happened, and here we are today. However, when one gets into the weeds of the evidence behind evolution, those holes like in the Swiss cheese are so apparent. They make this theory just what it is, a theory and a bad one at that, which does not belong in our schools at any level or any place else.

No matter how hard they try to pound this idea into our society and schools, the fact that God is in control of all things just cannot be dismissed. We need to place our trust in God, and His Son Jesus Christ, to help us defeat this movement and keep it away from our children.

7

Same but Different

One thing I can assure you, reader, is that I am no scientist, biologist, or botanist. Neither do I claim to be a theologian in any way. I have my shortcomings and inabilities due to my blindness and do not claim to know all things about all subjects. Nor do I like to be around people who think they know it all, as invariably they are going to stumble over themselves at some point. But it is just this inability on one person and the ability on another that make up the society of humans that God created.

At this point, I want us to take a trip back to our little friend the amoeba, the single cell we used as an example of what evolutionists think and believe we came from to develop into what we are today. If I remember one thing from my biology course in high school, it's that when one of these creations of God (and they are) splits in two to make two of them, they are identical. They have the same characteristics, structure, and cannot be told apart. Also, from one you can eventually have several amoebas, and they will all be the same.

Here again, we look at what the evolutionists want us to believe. First, the explosion, then the earth forms, then all the chemicals in perfect mixture come together, and voila, a single cell life is formed. Now I will be the first to admit and accept that there many more single cell organisms on earth than just our friend the amoeba. But it is the fact that they insist we evolved into what we are today from this microscopic source that is just not true.

The medical world is currently buzzing about the overuse of antibiotics, and some researchers are very concerned that due to this overuse, viruses may end up mutating and become immune or be completely unaffected by the antibiotic medicines in the future. Many of my facts and information in this book are a result of researching the endless data to be found on the internet. From that information, I have learned that a mutation is not the same as something developing several different kinds of itself.

We do have different strains of influenza, like the Victoria A, and the Hong Kong type. In my younger years, I had the Victoria A flu, and it was not a fun period of time for me.

Why we have these different kinds of germs, and why they even exist, is just another fact of life we have to accept, because the entrance of sin through Adam and Eve made it that way. This would come under the same reason why scorpions will lay into you one nasty sting, or snakes exist that can outright kill you.

This same line of thinking can be applied to more things than I can address in this chapter. We have so many plants and animals that are the same, yet they are also different, just like us humans. For example, there are many different types of tomato, from the small cherry tomato to the huge tomato called the beefsteak. There are several varieties of apples as well and pumpkins.

We have already written about the many different kinds of animals and species within each type, but even within them are similarities and differences. This also applies to humans, as we can be as diverse; yet, we are all the same.

My first full-time job was working at a meatpacking house in Manchester, Maryland. There I worked on the kill line,

Same but Different

where we slaughtered and cut up both beef and pork animals. Whether it was the pigs with their different colors of fur or the beef cattle with their various colors and types of hide, after the kill process, the dressed sides were placed into the cooler, and they all were the same.

No matter if the pig was white or black, a ham was a ham, and a pork loin was a pork loin. The cattle we killed could have been a black Angus, or some other member of the cattle family, but a T-bone steak came from the same animal as did a rib-eye steak.

The same is true with some of the plants we eat. Tomato sauce is tomato sauce, whether it is made from cherry tomatoes or the big boy beefsteak.

In the insect world, a bumblebee and a yellow jacket wasp will sting you just the same; however, they are entirely different kinds of bees and even perform a different task in the processes of life.

A coral snake and a king snake are both snakes; however, they are identified by the colors of rings on their bodies. A coral snake has its basic black coloring, with both yellow and red rings. The king snake is also basic black but with yellow and orange rings and is longer than the coral snake. The old saying from the west is so true, "red means dead."

The coral snake is deadly poisonous and can kill a full-grown man or woman in fifteen minutes; however, the king snake is harmless. Yet, the coral snake is the king snake's favorite meal. In fact, some ranchers like to have king snakes around to keep the coral snakes from striking and killing their cattle and horses.

In the fish world, a fish is not necessarily just another fish. The family favorite goldfish is as harmless as it can be, but a piranha of any size can make it a horrendous day for anyone or anything. One just swims around, and the other feeds on anything it can get hold of, reducing it to nothing but bones in minutes.

But, to every rule, there is always an exception. God must have decided to amuse Himself, when He created the duckbilled platypus found in rivers in Australia. Although officially identified as a mammal, this animal lays eggs for its young and even has a stinger that can inflict a nasty bit of pain.

The statement of the same but different applies to us humans as well. I am not talking about the fact that we speak different languages, or that some of us have blonde hair and other darker hair, or even that some of us are smaller in stature than others; although all of these things are true. No, I am referring to the fact that we are all the same inside from head to toe. Every human has a single head, two ears, two eyes, one mouth (which is enough for some people), two arms and two legs, and the trunk of the body from neck to the groin.

Have you ever just sat in a mall and watched the people walk by as they are shopping? Their manner of walking, reactions to items in the window, interaction with others in the mall, and even their facial features are just about as diverse as they can be; however, it is what is under that outer skin and appearance that makes us the same.

Further, each of us is unique, formed from a mating of our parents, but no two children of that mating will be the same. Each parent contributes a particular gene combination included inside of the woman's egg or the man's sperm. So the child will be a little bit of Mom and a little bit of Dad when they are born. However, child number one will not have the same gene mix as that of child number two, and on down the line. Some of my dearest friends are members of a family with ten kids. When you talk with them, you can always tell they are from that particular family, yet every one of them is different in their own way, from personalities to facial expressions, and six of them are boys while four of them are girls.

The fact that we are different because of our skin color is true in one sense but not in another. Just because one has black skin, like my African-American friends, or has a brown skin tone, like my Hispanic friends, or any other colored skin does not make them any less a human as anyone else, period. However, the fact that some of us have ailments others do not, like sickle cell anemia affecting only African-Americans, is also true. But, this is not the issue we are pursuing in this chapter.

We want to look under that skin, into the unseen body functions, where we can find so many similarities, even between men and women. When a surgeon opens a person's body to correct a medical problem, they will find what they are looking for, in the same place, in every person, be they male or female. In fact, except for the sexual parts of a male or female, our organs are in the same position in both sexes.

Today, medical science has grown to a point where organs are transplanted from one human into another, and it makes no difference if a male is getting a female organ, or if a female is getting a male organ. The medical team needs to determine that the organ and person receiving that organ have met the requirements for that organ to be accepted and function in the person's body.

In this same manner, medicine has proven to us that blood is blood, and everybody has red and white cells in that blood, and they perform the same function in the body. The only difference here is the types of blood, and whether they are positive or negative.

Unlike our little microscopic friend the amoeba, who creates another one of itself each time it splits, we humans create a new unique person each time we propagate ourselves. We may have the same parts, and in the same places; however, we are also different because we have a little of Mom and a little of Dad, we have totally different fingerprints, and our personalities are our own. Mom and Dad may like liver and onions as my parents did, but I could not stand the taste of either one and especially if they combined them with Brussel Sprouts. However, my mom and I like chicken gizzards, and my dad did not.

This idea of evolutionists that we all came off the same cookie-cutter assembly line, from that single cell something, is just plain untrue and baseless. Medical science alone disproves this theory based on all of the knowledge learned over the recent years alone. God made man and woman, and He told them to populate the earth, and we did twice.

Additionally, God has given unique talents and abilities to each person. We have a friend that can seem to fix or build anything you could think of, but I look at plumbing, and all I can say is, "Yep, that is a pipe." I have no idea how to work with pipe or to even fix plumbing, but my friend can without giving it a thought.

Others of us can make sewing machines sing and create our own clothing, yet others resort to the off-the-rack designs. Some can figure mathematics in their head, and others have a problem even with a calculator.

We are all unique, but we are still the same. God created us this way, and that is how it is A cookie-cutter theory is only useful for making chocolate chip cookies and does not apply in any manner to where we live, what lives around us, or who we are singularly or as a race of humans. It just is not that way!

Our individualities, combined with the talents God has given each of us and those of others is precisely why we are the same but different. If we all had the same talent of sewing, then who would repair our cars or fix the plumbing in our homes?

It is God's perfect plan of creation that has made our world as it is with each of us contributing our unique abilities, talents, understandings, and thoughts that make us able to address and resolve the problems life can and will bring into our lives.

8

Opposing Force

In the Bible, our opponent we call Satan is also known by several different names other than just the devil. He is known as Ababdon (Revelation 9:11), Adversary (1 Peter 5:8), Apollyon (Revelation 9:11), an Angel of Light (2 Corinthians 11:14), Anti-Christ (1 John 4:3), and the list goes on.

Created by God with the name Lucifer, he decided to take over heaven with disastrous results for him and those angels who chose to follow him. Ever since he was cast out of heaven (Isaiah 14:12-15; Revelation 12: 7-10), he has been the opposition to God and a real pain in our sides in so many ways.

How does Satan fit into the debate between evolution and creation? The very existence of sin on earth is due to his deception of Eve in the Garden of Eden (Genesis 3:1-5). Ever since the beginning, he has been causing trouble and making a mess of things all over the world.

He has been behind all of the reasons for wars, ruthless dictators who desired absolute rule like Adolf Hitler and Emperor Hirohito from World War II, murderous thugs like Joseph Stalin, the many terrorists of recent times, and the mafia kingpins over the years.

He has also been behind good marriages failing, people scamming others out of their life savings, and why people rob banks or other people for money. To put it simply, Lucifer is one huge pain in the neck!

Opposing Force

To say he makes a real mess of things would be the understatement of the year. Every time he can prevent someone from believing in Jesus Christ or makes one of us believers stumble in our faith so it affects someone from wanting to be a Christian, Satan dances the jig. We are instructed to resist the devil (James 4:7; 1 Peter 5:5), but there is not one of us who can say we did every time. Some of his temptations are quite appealing, and they can and will cause us to fall.

Trust me, reader, when I say that nobody can claim to have never sinned (Romans 3:23; 1 John 1:8-10). Whether you want to refer to it as a little white lie (which is just as much a sin as committing adultery or killing someone), or you have lived a life full of drugs and alcohol, fast women, or crime, all of us have done something sinful in our lifetime. It was fun while it lasted, but when the good times stopped, then we paid the price for our actions.

As an opposing force, he is a great deceiver in so many ways. This deception is not limited to causing us to sin alone but includes influencing people like the scientists who try to convince all of us that evolution is fact, when it is just a baseless theory that cannot be proven.

However, when a group like that school board I wrote about in the introduction decides to remove all things related to creation and insists that the students will be taught evolution only, we realize how much of an opposing force we are dealing with in this world. Remember, Satan's one goal is to keep all of us from even knowing about God and what His Son did on the cross to pay for our sins and lead us right into an eternal future in hell.

He already knows that he will be sent to hell eventually at the end of times, and with him will be all of the angels who followed him out of heaven, those that we call demons today. And like a big party, he tries to get as many there under the guise of the more the merrier. Believe me, hell will not be any party, nor is it anything like that depicted in Greek Mythology as having a river named Styx and a calm empty place (see my book *Time Witnessing*).

The things our opposing force will do to keep us from God have no limits. This is why I stated in the previous chapter, as food for thought, that I believe in UFOs and that he could have placed the dinosaur bones on earth to give science a basis to think that something else but God is in control of our universe.

He is the source of scientists taking the position that it just cannot be as simple as God said it, and it was so. No, there must be a much more complicated, complex reason requiring advanced analysis that has produced the thinking of evolution as the answer.

On many occasions, I have heard, and I am sure you have as well, someone commenting on the aftermath of a disaster like when a tornado or hurricane hits an area, people are killed, and homes and businesses are severely damaged. The first person they blame for the destruction is God.

God does not make the destruction. You may disagree, but the blame for the forces of these storms should not be directed at God. What our opposing force hopes for is that he can turn that person away from God and seal that person's future in hell.

After the destructive hurricane named Katrina hit New Orleans and the rest of that part of the USA, it was refreshing to learn that a now homeless man was sitting on the roadside reading his Bible. We do not and cannot understand God and His sovereign will for us. However, by faith, we can know that He will not allow anything to come into our lives that we cannot handle (James 1:2-8).

Now let's bring this back to our issue with the teaching of

evolution as fact. The opposition will use all the means available to get you away from God, including using your kids in school learning about a bad theory, and in doing so, helping deter your kids away from God and His creation. Many side issues can come out of this, including problems in the home between parents and children, leading the kids down the wrong avenues in life, etc. Satan does not care if you buy into evolution, the existence of dinosaurs or UFOs; all he wants to do is keep you away from God so he can take you along with him into hell. Trust me—you do not want to go there!

9

"In God Is Our Trust"

References: Fourth verse of the United States National Anthem.
History: The State of Tennessee versus John Thomas Scopes, July 21, 1925.

During the War of 1812, while a Prisoner of War on a British ship in the harbor of Baltimore, Maryland, local lawyer Francis Scott Key penned a poem that today are the words to our national anthem, "The Star Spangled Banner." The words that make up the title of this chapter are the final words from that poem, found at the end of the fourth verse.

In the original Pledge of Allegiance, the words "under God" were not part of that recitation. In the 1950s, Congress added these words, and then President Eisenhower signed the bill, making them part of the Pledge from that time onward.

Ever since that time, we have experienced different people and groups opposing anything relating to the acknowledgment of God's existence and influence. Courts have removed prayer and Bible reading from our schools, the public display of a cross and Ten Commandment monuments, and most recently, they tried to remove these words from the Pledge. Today, anything associated with Christianity is considered offensive, and now they are including using legal rulings from courts to remove God from our society.

The attempt to remove all things Christian, or any references to God, has been ongoing since the beginning. Multitudes of peoples have done many things worshipping false gods, also called idolatry. The very first commandment forbids this, as God demanded that He, and only He, be the recipient of man's worship.

Many peoples and tribes have practiced many things to appease their gods, resorting to child sacrifice to the fire gods in volcanoes, human sacrifice to please one or more gods, and going to war with others because they did not serve and worship their god. What all of these examples of worshipping other gods is missing is the fact that if you are not worshipping the one and only true God, then you are worshipping Satan.

All means are taken to deter one from the true God, and one of those actions is the promotion and demand to teach evolution in our schools. In our history reference for this chapter, a trial occurred in Dayton, Tennessee, where a substitute teacher was accused of teaching evolution.

In those days in Tennessee, there was a law called the "Butler Act," which forbade the teaching of evolution in publicly funded schools. The result of that trial led to the substitute teacher being convicted and given a small fine. Later, the conviction was overturned.

Times certainly have changed since the time of that trial on evolution. Today, it is just the opposite—the teaching of creation is being kept out by any means possible, including legally by local ordnances.

These actions rank right up there with denying graduates to mention God in their graduation ceremonies, prayer before a sporting event. It is getting even so personal as trying to prevent people from praying for their food in a public restaurant. This one has not happened to my wife and me yet, but I do believe the day is coming.

Creation Is a Science

Much is coming out of our government agencies that plainly remove God from the discussion. Those who continue participating in public prayer, displaying Christian symbols, etc. are being persecuted by the anti-Christian movement. It is getting so serious today that one cannot even wish another person a blessed day, without suffering a backlash from anti-Christian and atheistic organizations.

The scientists, who are pushing the theory of evolution as fact, are part of this anti-Christian, anti-Intelligent Design attitude in our schools. They are teaching, influencing, and deterring the college students today so that God and anything associated with the Bible are just automatically dismissed. Instead, all of this so-called research, analysis, and discoveries have replaced being able to accept that God created all things.

This teaching is also behind those who oppose anything about or referring to God, like the legal efforts to remove crosses, the flying of a Christian flag, a nativity scene at Christmas, Christmas itself, and plaques or monuments containing the Ten Commandments.

In the years leading up to World War II, the Nazis, led by Adolf Hitler and his henchmen like the Gestapo and Himmler's SS, sold the idea of their Nazi movement by influencing the youth. They took advantage of the youth being immature and impressionable and convinced them that they were the next generation of the "Master Race." By doing so, they were able to sell their poison and change the whole nation of Germany to their ideals and wishes. We know today how all that turned out, and the world still pays for that horrible period of time.

In the same way, Emperor Hirohito, recognized and worshipped as a god himself in Japan, influenced and caused his people to desire to conquer much of the far eastern countries that bordered the Pacific Ocean and the island nations in the

"In God Is Our Trust"

area as well. Many examples of Japanese soldiers and sailors choosing to die for the Emperor, instead of being captured by allied forces, showed this same devotion by impressing on the younger generation of Japan to show unbelievable allegiance to the death.

This is exactly what is happening when influential scientists, college professors, and even local school board members prevent our children to hear, know about, and learn of what God did in creating our world. Questions about where the birds, horses, and giraffes came from are squelched. Don't ask detailed questions because they do not want you to think and analyze why their theory is wrong and cannot be proven.

Millions were led to their deaths and eternity in hell because of Hitler and Hirohito, and our opposing force is using these so-called highly educated people to do the same thing now.

Beware parents and children, Satan and his demons are trying to keep you from even knowing about God and what His Son Jesus Christ did for you on the cross, and they want to take you with them to hell. Satan suffered a significant setback when Congress added "under God" to our Pledge; however, he is doubling his efforts to remove today what our Founding Fathers, and subsequent generations of leaders, put into place in our country.

Maybe the schools cannot lead you in a time of prayer, but that does not keep you from praying for yourself, your friends, and your parents to learn His will despite actions by others, and above all, that God will help you to stay strong in your faith. Read your Bible every day and know what God's Word says. We still have the Constitution in place in our country today, and as long as it remains, our personal freedoms to worship the one and only true God are still there too.

10

God's Control

Read the book of Jonah, Matthew 14:22-33, Luke 8:22-25.

In the mid-1980s, my parents were living in central Florida. During a visit to see them, I learned from my dad that Polk County, Florida, and a location in the middle of the African continent, were tied for the most lightning strikes in a year. Having lived in Texas for several years of my life, on hot, humid days, you learned to keep a watchful eye on the sky.

In the central part of the United States is an area that weather watchers call Tornado Alley. Here, if you see clouds building up and eventually forming what is referred to as an anvil top, you knew it was time to get the equipment in and head for the safety of a basement.

It is not just on dry land that you need to keep watch on the weather. Some of the most severe storms on earth develop over the open oceans and become hurricanes. In other parts of the world, they call them cyclones and typhoons, but they are all the same kind of storm. These storms contain very high winds, driving rain, and are just as destructive, if not more, as the tornadoes in the central part of the USA. As a young kid, I can remember looking out the window as a thunderstorm would be approaching and being fascinated by the lightning. The closer the storm came, I knew not to stay at the window long; but while it was still safe, I looked on with awe.

God's Control

When I got older and became a homeowner myself, I looked upon incoming storms with concern and often would take a moment to pray for God's safety on our home and my family. Why? Simple, He is in control of all things on earth, including a thunderstorm. In the reading I have listed for this chapter, you will read about three stories from the Bible, where God and Jesus demonstrated their complete control of all things.

In the story of Jonah, God caused a severe storm to strike the boat Jonah was in, and after the sailors tossed him overboard, the rains and wind stopped immediately. Then God caused a big fish to swallow Jonah and later spit him out onto the shoreline. Finally, God showed Jonah a lesson by growing a shade vine for him and then killed it with a little worm. God showed Jonah that He was in control of all things. Jonah's fears were no match for what God could do for Jonah and for the people in Nineveh, located near modern-day Mosul, Iraq, where Jonah was called to bring the word of God.

In Matthew and Luke's accounts, Jesus showed the disciples that He was God as well. As the Son of God, Jesus shared the same power over all things and stilled raging storms by s simple spoken word or action. Not a single thing happens on earth that God does not know about it and permits or restrains it, according to His sovereign will.

Many stories have been told of people praying to God to deliver them from a tornado threat or some other kind of weather-related disaster, and God provided a miracle. Homes on either side were destroyed, but the home where the residents were praying was spared without a scratch.

However, God does not always say yes to our petitions, and we suffer loss. The Bible does tell us that the rain falls on the just as well as the unjust, so we will not always be spared. This fact comes from the Bible reference I provided in a previous chapter, where God will not allow to come upon us what we cannot handle.

This fact of God's complete control does not just apply to weather conditions. It is very evident in our everyday lives. He allows thing to happen to test our faith in Him, whether we will put our trust in Him, and to teach us patience to wait on Him to answer our prayers as He sees fit. We will not always like how He answers our prayers because sometimes He does say no; however, He will always answer us in the way that is best for us in the long run. Remember, He knows the future and what is waiting for each of us tomorrow, next week, next year, and farther in the future. I can look back on God's decision in my life when I was not pleased with Him at all; however, now years later, I see why it occurred and that it was best for me in the future.

How can our children getting evolution shoved down their throats be good for them in the future? I am not God, and I will not answer for Him, but it just might be to help them increase their faith here and now, as well in the future. In biblical terms, nothing will toughen you up better than a good testing by God.

When we are first born again and are like babies in God's Word, we cannot handle serious testing. As we grow in our knowledge of the Bible and a few rough times come and go, God prepares us for what He already knows will come our way down the road of life. He gives us that thick skin needed to handle those situations.

When I was in school and was bullied for one reason or another, I always thought the idea of turning the other cheek was nuts. Mom and Dad would always tell me just to walk away, but I cannot remember one time that ever worked, as the bully would chase me down and lay into me. I must admit that after a while of always getting the wrong end of this deal, a day came

God's Control

when I stood my ground, and someone else had the privilege of looking up at me for once. I had enough, and it was time for a reaction to their action.

The same goes for wrongs we experience in life. Sure, the first step is to pray to God about the situation, even though He already knows about it in detail. Next, look for His will in what you should or should not do about the situation. Finally, follow His will in resolving the situation. If it is in His will, it will not go wrong!

God will allow issues, difficulties, and sorrows to come into our lives to strengthen and increase our faith in Him and to prove to us that there is not a thing He cannot handle or will not be in control of from the start. When Satan tries to tear us up by bringing sorrow into our lives, we can always remember that he cannot do anything to us that God will not permit and knows we can handle. Because of this fact, we have old boy Satan beat before he starts. This should not make us cocky, though, because the testing God has permitted could hurt a little, so keep the issue in perspective too.

We need to apply this information to our situation with a school board that will not allow Intelligent Design to be taught in the schools we pay property taxes to operate. Do not stop paying taxes because you will end up with a much bigger problem than a bad school curriculum. Instead, let those who levy that tax upon you know just how you want the money spent.

Start your line of attack by bringing it before God in prayer. Get others of like mind together and brainstorm the issue, ideas, and possible actions. The more the merrier is a good thing here, because if the elected officials see a major sized group of voters opposed to an issue, they better plan on changing or face removal at the next time their seat is up for re-election. Make sure they know that too.

11

God's Will

Read Matthew 7:7-8, Luke 11:9-10, Revelation 3:20.

We are now going to go to the next step in this book and expand on what we just discussed in the previous chapter. One question you may have already asked is just how do we know God's will for our personal lives and in dealing with things in our public lives?

There is no cookie-cutter answer to this question because each issue is different and unique to each person and their personalities. Sometimes good old common sense will show you God's will in the matter, but it is those things where there is a large amount of fogginess and uncertainty that makes knowing what God wants us to do hard to determine. Lots of prayer, reading and studying the Bible, and sharing with others might be needed to learn this answer, and that is exactly where we are going now. We are going to take a trip through several steps in knowing God's will, and just how to handle it once we have that answer.

Any motivational speaker worth his salt will lead his audience through steps in accomplishing a goal, solving a problem, or improving themselves. Hopefully, I will help you to this point in knowing God's will, and it all starts with having those personal times of devotions and prayer with God. If you leave God out of the mix, you are already two strikes down before you

God's Will

start, and it will not take much to achieve that third strike.

If you feel God desires you take part in or lead an action as a result of your time spent with Him and His Word, the Bible, then it is time for the following steps to be taken and followed through with to the end.

STEP 1 – Organize

Something that is quite prominent in our lives today is organizations called Political Action Committees (PACs). An individual or a group of people, with like-minded desires and goals, will come together and form a PAC to help bring about their desired political result.

They vary from a person who wishes to pursue an elected office, like that of the presidency, or a movement like those who oppose abortion. No matter what their goal is, they began as a person with an idea or one who wanted to make a change in how things are going in the world today.

This is the first step you want to take in addressing the issue or problem at hand. You might want to start with the others who attend your church, are part of a club you belong to, or are your friends and neighbors. See how others view the situation, if they do or do not like how things are going, and try to form a group that wishes to change things.

Going after a change on your own will not make any impression on anybody, especially if those whom you are trying to make a change with are elected officials. They will have no concern about a person with only one vote.

Do not be concerned about diversity with those you get to join your cause. In fact, you want diverse ideas to help mold the group into a common cause and goal. It may not always be possible, but getting a professional like a lawyer, a local elected official, or some other prominent person into your group can and will be quite helpful.

The change you wish to make may not make much of an impression on those who are the target of your desired change if they are only hearing something from Mr. John or Ms. Jane Q. Public, but they might sit up straight if they are being addressed by someone of note and influence in the community.

Once you have formed a group who want this change, it is time to sit down and organize. Elect a leader of the group, who is willing to be the spokesperson for the group. You will need a secretary or recorder to keep notes or minutes from each meeting to show what was discussed and where the group stands on that point at the next meeting. Depending on the action you are pursuing, a treasurer may also need to be appointed, and an account for keeping the funds established at a local bank.

Finally, I would strongly suggest you include a pastor or elder from a church in the area that is in support of your cause. Keep God in the mix, and this is a perfect way to do so.

Upon completion of this first step, you need to agree upon when the group will meet, such as a particular evening, at a certain time acceptable to all, and where the meetings can and will be held. If your church or another church in the area is part of your cause, ask them if meetings can be held in a room at the church. Apart from not feeling well or that your work has you out of town at that time, make all possible efforts not to miss a single meeting.

STEP 2 – Discuss and Brainstorm

Let's look back at the point that all of us are unique in our own way and are not the same as chocolate chip cookies on an assembly line. This is where diversity in the group will be an advantage. Yes, differing views could get heated at times, but this is where your leader needs to keep things civil and on the point

God's Will

being discussed and working on that goal for change.

Each person should also agree to be civil in their participation, and this is where a document of agreement, like a covenant that establishes in writing what the group stands for and has been created for, can seal and help mold the group to the common cause.

You must never lose focus on the reason you formed your group to begin with, or you might as well simply fold up and be on your way. Without that goal in front of you at all times, the discussion can go off in a direction that has nothing to do with the problem. As a result, you will have accomplished nothing and wasted the time of those attending the meeting. Here again, the leader must keep the group on point and intercede when things start to drift off point.

Do not be afraid to challenge each other on this point as well, as you may feel that what one person is bringing up has nothing to do with your cause. However, hear them out as they may know something the group was not aware of that just might make their information very much involved in the issue being dealt with for change.

Here is a critical point. Do not meet once or twice and then go after trying to make the change you desire. Take time to meet several times, really get into the weeds of the problem, understand who you will be dealing with, and why they feel that what they have established or done is in the best interest of the area.

Knowing what those who oppose you stand for, who they are, and the reasons behind their position is so essential. To debate someone, you need to know something about the subject at hand, because without this knowledge, you will definitely get nowhere in your opposition and in the arguments you bring before them.

Creation Is a Science

If the organization you are opposing meets publicly, attend several meetings and look for wrinkles in their proverbial armor, and if there are any differing opinions on their board or committee. Then share your intelligence at the next meeting and plan your manner of presenting your opposition to the established ruling or ordinance by giving reasons why it should be changed.

On this point, you may want to select sub-committees to handle particular areas of the issue. One could be the intelligence group who attend the opposition's meetings and take notes for the group. Another may work on refining what you feel should be how things are handled and why. Be creative and never think you have enough information or intelligence. It is much better to have more information than you need, rather than be in a position of needing more information and not having it to review.

Now that you have discussed the issue or problem in detail and have done your research (which should be ongoing during the entire process), attended some meetings, and gathered your intelligence as well as the needed homework, it is time to take this information and do the hard part of this step—brainstorming.

If possible, a round table discussion addressing the what ifs, if we did this or thats, information on how the opposition handles people with differing opinions, and any other data that would be helpful in preparing your presentation should be laid out for all to hear and address. Do not be afraid of disagreements; just address each so you can work out the best way to get the change you want made on the issue at hand.

It is so important that the leader of your group is fully versed on the issue, why the situation even exists, what the group wants changed, and most importantly, how to present it to get the desired change.

When and only when, the group feels it is ready to make the case for change, it is time for your group to request time on the agenda of the board or committee's next meeting. Check your calendars and make sure all or as many as possible can attend. Also, the designated spokesperson for your group must agree that he or she is ready to make the presentation. If they have any doubts at all, get them resolved prior to requesting the time. Settle any existing disagreements, differing views, and prepare to come to the meeting as a group in total support of what is presented to the board or committee.

Finally, before attending the meeting, take time to get on those knees and ask God to help you, guide you, and even give the spokesperson the words they need to make the presentation before this organization. There is no sense in doing all this work and not keeping God in the center of all the planning. Remember, the Apostle Paul stated that if God is for us, who can be against us (Romans 8:31).

STEP 3 – Request and Present

After all the homework, intelligence, and needed information have been assembled, and all are in agreement that your group is ready to present your case for change, it is time for you to make a formal request to be scheduled onto the board or committee's next meeting agenda. Most organizations do not allow you just to walk in and ask to be recognized. They will make your request part of their next meeting agenda, and that request will include the reason for your presentation.

At least two of your group's membership should go to the appropriate office to apply for the request and make known to the office that this is not a lone wolf complaint. Make sure those members understand that saying no to your request is not an answer or is in any way acceptable.

If, by any chance, this publicly elected board chooses to deny your request, they must tell you why in writing. Saying they just do not want to hear your presentation is not acceptable, and you should challenge why you cannot exercise your freedom of expression to that board. On this point is where some legal help can make a difference and cause the board not to say no, or for sure make them reconsider their decision.

Make sure to have one final meeting before the date of your scheduled presentation, review what will be said, and perhaps even anticipate some questions or responses that may be negative. Conclude the meeting in prayer, asking for God help and intervention.

Then in the privacy of your own homes, be sure to keep your prayer line open to God, stay in touch with your fellow group members, and seek out others who did not or could not participate to let them know about the meeting. Although they could not participate, it does not mean they might not be in total agreement, and they might try to attend the meeting to support your efforts on their behalf as well as your own.

On the day and time of the meeting, do not show up like some kind of ragtag group of hippies or disheveled folks. Try to come in at least what is called casual dress, and let those who you are coming to present your feelings and desires to know that you are not just a bunch of bums that do not like something. These meetings are not formal affairs, so unless you choose to, the wearing of a suit and tie for men, and a high-quality dress for women are not necessary or expected.

Lastly, before the meeting begins, have one more time of prayer as a group, and you might even want to lay hands on the person who will be acting as your spokesperson.

Your spokesperson can either read from a prepared state-

God's Will

ment, so as to not miss any points the group wishes to bring before the meeting, or they can simply express the feelings of the group on your issue. This may be a choice of your spokesperson, and what manner they feel more comfortable in presenting the requested change.

Then be prepared for numerous questions, requests for clarification, and just plain negative responses. However, do not accept any comments that can be considered as profane (be ready to tell the person who did just how you feel about their manner of speaking in a public forum).

If your spokesperson needs to obtain some clarification from the group, be ready to advise them on how you desire that they respond to the question. Remember, you are attending in support of your group's desire for change, so be ready to help make your point clear and precise, leaving no doubt in the minds of the board of just why you feel a change must be made to the existing situation, ruling, or ordinance.

Following your presentation, the board may choose to consider your points and work on a response. They can table the discussion to the next meeting, but unless they feel strongly about their action in the past, it is very doubtful that you will get a decision from that organization on that same night.

Keep in contact with the board, find out if they plan to address your issue soon; however, until you get a response from them, do not miss a single meeting in the future until you do get an answer. Commit the evening's results to God, and let Him work in ways we cannot, and pray that the board will change the situation. Stay with it until the end, and if the result is not acceptable, then we need to take the next step in this process.

STEP 4 – Volunteer and Remove

After all the hours of research, planning, meetings, and discussions, presenting your request for change, if you receive a negative response, where do you go from here? No matter what the organization is, those who serve on the board are probably elected either publicly or within the organization itself. If they will not budge, then it is time for them to get the boot.

Your group needs to meet and discuss, analyze the board's response and reason for the negative answer, and decide what steps you want to take to get the changes made that are desired. If you have come this far, now is not the time to excuse yourself from the group. Instead, it is time for one or more members to volunteer to initiate the necessary actions to run against the sitting board members and pursue removing them at the time of the next election cycle.

In the area where I live, publicly elected boards usually have half of the board up for re-election every two years, but this differs from board to board. Most boards are made up of an odd number of members, with the chairman or president serving as the tie-breaker vote. With this knowledge, now your group needs to get the necessary volunteers required to maybe remove the members up for re-election, perhaps removing them even in the primary election cycle.

For example, if the board is made up of seven members, and three of them are up for re-election in the next cycle, your group should try to get six or more to get their names on the primary ballot, or as many as would be needed to give these members the boot before the general election held each November.

If the primary results do not get some or all of them removed, make sure enough of those on your side are on the ballot in November to remove them at that time. Then in two years, repeat this same process until you have removed those who will

God's Will

not change, and those of you who do get elected can at that time make the changes that need to be made, and above all glorify God.

Here again, is where you need to know God's will for you. If God wants you to serve on that board, He will make sure you get on it too. However, you must be willing to take that step and file the proper documents to get your name on the ballot. Make it clear to the voters that you will make a change, and it will be to God's glory for the betterment of the area.

Be absolutely sure you can fulfill the position for the term designated. Make sure you are allowed to run for an elected office. While I was an employee of the U.S. Government, the Hatch Act prevented me from running for an elected office, period.

Maybe your work is always at night, which would keep you from attending board meetings, then you need to take that into consideration. If you travel for your work often, this would affect your attendance as well. Bottom line, if you choose to take this step, be sure you can, are willing, and fully intend to fulfill the requirements of the office, so help you God.

Another thing you must consider is that you are qualified to even be a part of the resolution. I have referred to the evolution versus creation problem in a local school district several times. There is not one thing I can do about it because I do not live in that school district. If you know about it but cannot be part of the resolution, then become a prayer supporter. Ask God to help those who do live in that district make a change that will allow the students to know and learn about the truth of how we exist today.

I cannot emphasize enough the need for bringing your issue to God in prayer. One very important fact I have learned from the past is that God can change situations and opinions when all of our efforts have failed. Also, do not limit your abilities to make this issue public. Write letters to the editor of the local newspaper, expose the issue at town hall venues, and write or address the issue with your State or Federal elected representatives.

If it is a court decision you are opposing (like in this school district), pray first, then seek out some legal representation to appeal the decision. In the USA, there is free legal representation available from the Alliance Defending Freedom (ADF) or the American Center for Law and Justice (ACLJ).

No matter what, never stop that line of prayers to God, asking for His will and His intervention. Remember, God wants us to ask Him for His help, so ask, seek, and knock for it (Deuteronomy 4:29; Jeremiah 29:13; Matthew 7:7; and Luke 11:9).

12

PTO Meetings

In today's schools, parents, students, and teachers alike are all dealing with many adverse situations inside of the administrations and district boards., not only in the teaching of evolution and preventing any instruction on creation. We also have the removal of Ten Commandments plaques from the school premises and a nasty issue of the introduction of Common Core.

The biggest problem the area Parent Teacher Organizations (PTOs) are experiencing comes from board members and administrators who do not listen to the taxpayers but are listening and following the directions of our government's endless regulations and the influence of the liberal folks referred to as Social Progressives (SPs).

The Federal Courts, school boards, and administrators are preventing and removing anything even closely associated with God, Jesus Christ, or anything Christian at all. They are keeping this from the students because they feel it will adversely affect them.

Yet, you hear of more and more schools allowing things related to the religion of Islam to enter schools. Recently, a news report told of a school in New York that had the students reciting the Pledge of Allegiance in Arabic. Others were making accommodations for Muslim students to take time out of the school day to pray to Mecca, including making space for them to lay out their prayer rugs.

The 1st Amendment to the Constitution does protect the right of a citizen to worship as they wish; however, the SCOTUS ruling of 1963, which removed prayer and Bible reading from the schools, also applies equally to all religious activities, or it applies to none of them.

If a Christian student cannot bow his or her head and pray over their food or to do well in a test, then why can Muslims students take time out of the school day and pray to Allah (who is Satan just by another name)? This issue is done because either all can or none can, period.

In accordance with the Constitution, the courts, including SCOTUS, are only to enforce the law and/or rule if a certain legislative action is supported by the Constitution. What they cannot do, but the 1963 decision is being viewed as, is to make law.

This responsibility belongs only to the legislative branch of government we call Congress (see the United States Constitution, Article I, Section 8). The 1963 ruling is not law, and if seriously challenged, it cannot be enforced.

When it comes to the curriculum our students are taught in school, allowing a board to decide what will and what will not be presented is plain wrong. Nor should such decisions be left to the courts. Parents and teachers alike should have some input to the material, contents of the school books, and the way a subject can and will be taught.

This brings us to a very big issue in schools today, and that is the introduction of Common Core. So far, this teaching tool, manner of teaching, and government regulated curriculum involve only English, History in some cases, and Mathematics, as of the writing of this book. But, this is too far already, as Common Core takes away the diversity of the students, the

PTO Meetings

speed or lack thereof at which they learn, and places all students into its own type of cookie-cutter teaching method. Test scores are all equal, and there is no place or allowance for students that are special needs kids, are slower at learning, and may not be exactly keeping up with the rest of the students.

Just some of the cons for adopting Common Core are that a correct answer is not just accepted, but the student must defend it as well. I guess that if a student says that 2+2=4, that is not good enough? Common Core requires this equation to be listed as 1+1+1+1=4, because the student must establish how they achieved the number 2 to start within the math problem. They have to come up with a reasonable defense for the number 4 being the answer.

Another con is that all tests will be standardized, nationwide, so students in inner-city Chicago, Los Angeles, and New York City, will have to take the same test as students in Boise, Idaho; Santa Fe, New Mexico; and Huntsville, Alabama.

On the English side of the coin, Common Core makes little, if any, concessions for the Hispanic community. A student who may have a language issue and their first language at home is Spanish, will be expected to perform at the same standard as students who speak English as their first language.

Somewhere down the line, I lost where Common Core will allow teachers to work with slower students, grade tests based on the answers given, and that many students will just give up trying due to their inability to comprehend at the same speed of others, or their language background keeps them from understanding as quickly as others. Here you run into the danger of school dropouts, and this will threaten that student's future in many ways.

Many states have just plain said no to Common Core, like my beloved Texas, as well as Virginia, Alaska, Indiana,

Oklahoma, and Nebraska. I see this method of teaching as a threat to our kids in a spiritual manner too. The youth are, by nature, very impressionable and easily swayed. If their education is being limited by demanding what they may fall short of, then their ability to understand and discern their need for God in their lives is threatened as well.

I must admit that my feelings toward homeschooling, or the operation of church-owned schools, have greatly changed. When I was still in school, a local church operated its own school, and the kids that came out of that school were naive beyond belief on the issues and matters of life that were waiting for them in the real world.

So out of touch were those kids that I took serious pity upon them. If the instructions your student gets shelters them from the realities of the world, you need to make a change in the curriculum and teaching methods as they will have no clue how to handle those who are influenced by the world's desires and actions.

Today, private schools have made many changes and improvements so kids are not so naive but are prepared. With the establishment of Christian schools that serve a particular area, instead of a local church's programs, they can be ready to face the world at face value, deal with sinful and ungodly actions taken toward them, and have a good foundation in their faith in God.

The same can be said of those who choose to home school their kids. Yes, we are not supposed to be part of the world, but they should be prepared to face what the world has to offer, both good and bad.

Finally, even Christian kids do not fit into a cookie-cutter society. In our church, we have programs for special needs kids that give them a manner of learning about Jesus yet we present

PTO Meetings

it in the best way for them to understand and learn. This kind of program is also beneficial to the parents of these kids, as the classes give them a short break from the child so they can hear the message from God's Word. They can realize a positive result when their child, who has difficulties with simple things, proclaims his or her friendship with Jesus.

You have never heard "Jesus Loves Me" sung better than when a small group of special needs kids does it by holding up signs, and in their own way, by sound. Many a tear has fallen from this old dude on those occasions.

Our schools should not be operated in accordance with regulations from Washington, D.C. The states and the local school boards should be the determining level of government that decides what will be taught, how it will be taught, and what will be or not be allowed within the campuses of the schools.

These decisions must be influenced by how the parents and teachers desire the students to be instructed, and whether they can learn about something like creation or pray openly if they so desire. God should not ever be removed from them. You see, the kids have the same rights under the Constitution as we adults do, and if they desire to thank God for their food, helping in a test, or for bringing them to that point when they graduate, they should be allowed to do so and without any actions taken against them.

13

The Church in Education

Read Psalms 32:8, Proverbs 1:7-8, 8:33, 22:6, Luke 6:40, and Ephesians 6:4

Many times during my Dad's forty-five-year career as a minister, he would have occasion to lead in a baby dedication service. In the church my wife and I now attend, this same baby dedication service is held. In both cases, it would end with a charge to the congregation to assist the new parents in teaching the child in the ways and instructions given in the Bible.

It is a fact that God holds the parents directly responsible for the proper upbringing of the baby He has blessed them with, including and especially in the manner and instructions set forth in the Bible. Also, the church has a share in this responsibility too.

Our pastor just completed a series titled "We Are the Church." In this several week series, he brought out how the people in the church building are "the Church," and it is not the building. Among his many points during these weeks, he included how the congregation shares in the responsibility and duty to help train and instruct the children in what and who God is and what Jesus Christ did for us on the cross.

From the ladies who care for the infants and toddlers, up to the Sunday School teachers for the high school and college-aged young adults, he emphasized that "the Church" can and

The Church in Education

should be part of this upbringing to the glory of God.

This part does not stop within the walls of the church building. It can and should spill out into the homes and businesses, and especially the area schools. Some long-time friends of my family, and now retired missionaries, are involved in the Child Evangelism Fellowship (CEF) program at one of our local elementary schools. In these after-school Bible study and teaching programs, they provide these youngsters with the basics of the Bible and their need to accept Jesus Christ as their Savior.

Others in our church are actual teachers in the schools and do not restrict themselves from expressing their faith in front of the kids. However, the movement to stop these actions and limit what can or cannot be said in the classrooms along with the future of Bible classes in public buildings is starting to be felt in our area of central Pennsylvania.

When a school board or the courts decides to stop prayers before sporting events, Baccalaureate services as part of the graduation process, allowing Bible study classes after school hours, and even determining if creation will or will not be taught in the schools is when members of the congregation, who live within the area that district serves, need to take action. The church congregation as a whole needs to commit this issue to prayer both collectively and in the privacy of their homes.

When I graduated from high school in 1972, my dad led the Baccalaureate service. Sure, he did it because I was part of the class, but it was also the church he served at that time being involved in the functions of the schools. Although I do not remember every word Dad said that evening, I know that he pulled no punches in telling my classmates, and those attending the service, about Jesus Christ and the need we had of accepting Him as our Savior. In addition, he told us how Jesus, as Lord of our lives, can and will help us through the hills and valleys that life will bring from time to time.

I remember so well how many of the parents and students were very upset at the Federal Court and their local school board for removing creation from the curriculum and allowing only evolution to be taught as fact. The local television stations covered this controversial decision in that district, and then it just died from public view. Instead, the local church congregations should have come together, attended the next board meeting, and raised the roof on this denial of teaching creation in their district's public schools.

Some people opposed the teaching of evolution and rejected any idea of allowing both creation and evolution to be taught. They favored just letting the students decide which one was correct and the other just plain baseless. I believe that I have made it quite clear from the evidence I provided in the first part of this book, which one is true, and which one is baseless.

We have to accept that there are folks in the world just as opposed to creation being in the school as Christians are to evolution. Here is where we have to look at the big picture and focus on getting creation to the students.

As Soldiers of the Cross, when we do sin (and we all do), Satan just loves to drive into that crack in our Christian armor with an M1 tank and try to take us down so that we are no longer a symbol and example of what a Christian should be in life. We can use this very same tactic to defeat Satan and his demons by getting the teaching of creation into the school. Even though it will be presented in the same manner as evolution, in this way the students get to hear and know about how God did create the universe. God will use that inlet of His creation to challenge and bring students into a position to accept Him as their God.

The Church in Education

Taking on Satan can sometimes require a bit of covert actions on our part; and with God's help, we will get to drive our M1 tank into the curriculum of the school. This idea is not a compromise in any way, because the alternative keeps the students from hearing about God. We need to jump upon any way of getting God into our schools.

Churches can help sponsor an event at the school that does not necessarily have to be purely Christian oriented. Many of our Founding Fathers were Christians and openly expressed their faith in the early years of our nation. So being involved in the celebration of Presidents Day in February could be an opening to teach about Presidents Washington and Lincoln, both of whom are documented to have acknowledged their faith in God.

Another excellent event to be part of as a church with the schools is on the September day when Christian students gather around the flag pole of the school and pray for our nation, their fellow students, and that God would help them to be good witnesses for Him at school.

Then there are the holidays of Thanksgiving and Christmas. Your church can help bring about the understanding of the Pilgrims eating with the Indians and how God was in the middle of that event. And at the special event of Christmas, they can emphasize the reason for the season.

In today's world, you and the church will get nowhere in getting God back into the schools if all we do is pound the pulpits with fire and brimstone, scream about being left out like a bunch of banty roosters. Instead, we need to do that brainstorming I wrote about earlier and come up with some ideas that the school district would allow you to sponsor outright, or be a participant in, and thereby get your proverbial foot in the door.

We need to be just as cunning as a lioness on the hunt, yet

up front, when we plan on getting God back into the schools. Taking on the schools as General Robert E. Lee did against the Union Army at Gettysburg, is not the way, because all we will get is either a backlash or an outright rejection of our intended actions. Instead, we need to use the Union Army's tactic of subtle actions, soft intentions, that get us in the door, and then we can just let God work.

If your church has a committee dedicated to the oversight of the Christian education inside the walls, maybe it can expand its work to matters outside as well. Did you know that there is no such thing as the Separation of Church and State? It is not in the Constitution anywhere. So when anti-Christian and atheist organizations claim it is unconstitutional to have a nativity scene on public land, they are just blowing smoke and have no basis for their claim.

With that in mind, ask if you can set up a Christmas display in the school lobby, along with a Christmas tree, at no cost to the school at all. Maybe the school needs some new equipment that you could provide for them and get your name in the school on the plate that shows who gave the equipment to the district.

Getting good books in the library is always a good idea. Have a sub-committee of your education leadership sit down and come up with ideas on how you can get involved in the school and look for that opening that will get God back where He is so desperately needed.

One idea that is always a hit, and is rarely ever denied, is providing food at a sporting event at the school. See if you can set up a hot dog and burger stand at every home game during the football season. If approved, you can put up a tent, or have someone build you a more structurally sound shed or shack; and make sure you have some kind of banner or sign showing who is sponsoring and operating the food stand. Do not do anything

The Church in Education

the district says is unacceptable, but do all you can to get your name out there to let people know that your church cares, and God does too.

Maybe to get the shack built, the church can provide the wood to the school, and the industrial arts students learning woodworking can build it for you, as a joint venture between the school and your church. Let them paint it in the school colors and get it placed near the football field, where you can set up shop, feed the masses, and show God's love to all you come into contact with at the game. God does work in mysterious ways, so do not limit Him in how you can make a dent in the school armor and get Him back into the school.

14

Taking Down Evolution

In one of the founding documents of the United States, the Declaration of Independence, will be found the word "Creator." Many of the Founding Fathers who were believers in God (known as Deists) could be found in church services on Sundays, even during the Revolutionary War period.

Unlike many others, the author of this document, Thomas Jefferson, was not what we would call a believer in the truest sense, but he did acknowledge the existence of God. From what I have learned about him, I genuinely believe even he would be very upset to know what is being forced upon our school students today. If these men were in charge today, creation would be in our schools, and the theory of evolution would be removed and banned.

So how have we regressed so far to the point that our federal courts and school boards are removing creation and forcing evolution to be taught as fact? In a biblical sense, one word: sin. In a general sense, we have simply rejected the idea that there is even a God and that He simply commanded it to be and our world began. The basis of this unbelief is the same word: sin.

This unbelief results in the government restrictions on what can or cannot be said in public, like a prayer to numerous organizations attacking everything Christian and preventing our children from knowing the truth about God and His creation.

In this book, we have looked at in detail what scientists

would have us believe and try to establish as fact—the bad theory of evolution. I have endeavored to refute their claims with simple common sense, plain truths, well-known facts of nature, and what is stated in the Bible. Before I started this book, I knew evolution was a baseless theory, and now I hope you have all the evidence you need to say the same thing.

If schools want to teach our children about science and physics, that is fine, as long as what they teach are known facts. Evolution is just a wild guess, made to deny the existence of God.

I am just an ordinary person, blind as a bat (another creation of God), who utilized basic facts and the results of simple research online. I believe with the help of my God, I totally debunked this theory. I used before, and I am using again, the illustration that evolution has more holes in its content than Swiss cheese, and it is thinner in basis than a strip of old microfilm. Yet, science would cram this down our student's throats, claim it as fact, and deny and prevent them from knowing anything about God and His creation.

Looking back on what I have provided as information, facts, suggestions, and ideas of how to change what may be facing your students in school, I thought of one more idea that has worked in the past and will work again.

You can initiate a petition drive in your area to have a proposition placed onto the next ballot that, if approved, would force the school board to allow creation into the school curriculum. Make sure the proposition would be considered binding to the results of the vote; and if approved, that the schools would start including biblical facts immediately.

Another thing I want to make crystal clear is that I am not suggesting we remove science, chemistry, and physics from schools. Quite the contrary, because it is our knowledge of these various studies that help us in many ways today. We can thank chemistry for so many conveniences in our homes, cars, and everyday living, for the invention of plastics, medicines that cure our illnesses, and on the list could go for miles of pages.

Physics has given us an understanding of our weather, predicting storms and telling us when to take cover. Along with the sciences associated with space travel, the satellites help warn us of developing dangers. The problem is when science just plainly dismisses God's part in all that we have, the raw materials He provides us with, and how we can use them for our betterment. That is when God allows failures, difficulties, and even sorrows to come into the lives of us humans.

The bottom line of these problems can be traced back to people of advanced education who want to keep God out of the picture. Until the temptation of Eve in the Garden of Eden, and subsequently that of Adam, God had created a world without sin, disease, or dangers.

Ever since that time, all of us have been born with this sin nature, but we can inhibit that part of our makeup by focusing on God, what His Son Jesus Christ did for us on that Roman cross, and asking Him to be the Savior of our lives. It is just that simple, but Satan and his demons do not want you to know this fact. They would make you think that becoming a Christian means no more fun, you will have to walk around acting like a monk, and you would not be able to enjoy the happiness of life. Nothing could be farther from the truth because the primary joy of believing in God and accepting His Son as Savior is the guarantee of your heavenly home.

You have God to turn to when the road is not so smooth, and others try to take away from you what is yours to have and enjoy. When others attempt to remove God from your children in school, He will be your guide to make things right, and by our trusting Him to do so, Satan and his demons face another defeat.

We need to bring this rather long motivational and instructional book to a close. Knowing that Satan is continually doing all he can to mess up our lives by keeping God away from our kids and confusing the world with theories that are just plain wild guesses. He hopes to make you one of his co-inhabitants in hell and keep you from God and His glories in heaven.

Instead, we need to trust in God, and with His help make things different where we work, where we live, where our kids go to school, and even in our government activities on the federal, state, and local levels. I have waved the Red, White, and Blue; however, I am also waving the fact of the ultimate sacrifice for all of us on a cross long ago.

If you want to get rid of these things that are detrimental in your life, you must start with that person you see in the mirror every morning. If things are not right with you, you will not get anything done outside of your home.

For us to take down any adversities, be they evolution in our schools, unfair laws that restrict our freedom to worship God, or denying our freedoms of expression, we need Jesus Christ in our personal lives, corporate lives as a community, and within the walls of our churches. God must be at the center of those governmental activities that affect all of us every day. Until this happens, we will continue to struggle with our sin, the sinful acts of others, and face disappointments and sorrows.

The best piece of advice I have ever received is that if I keep God at the center of everything I do, say, pursue, desire, and work to earn, He will give it all to me. However, if I try to obtain those things I want, lust for, and seek—riches of one kind or another—He will not grant them to me because He knows the future and how they will affect my service for Him.

Whatever it is you are trying to change, correct, and improve, it will go much smoother if you have God in the middle of all your efforts. Remember, even soldiers with all of their weapons, armor, and equipment still do intelligence gathering before attacking the enemy. So do your homework, learn about your adversary, and above all, look to God to guide you in all things. Trust me, when God is on your side, Satan loses every time.

15

Creation A to Z

The beginning chapters of Genesis tell us that God created all creatures on the land, in the air, and in the sea. To put this in more concrete terms, God created everything from the aardvark to the zebra and everything in between, including all the plants found all over the world. I found it most difficult to end this book without looking again at God's amazing creations. As I stated earlier, one could wonder why He created some of the creatures, like the scorpion, black widow spider, and the various venomous snakes and sea creatures.

Each of them has their part in everyday life on earth. This includes us humans, from plowing the fields and planting crops to feed the populations of the earth, to harvesting trees and iron ore for the building of our homes and businesses. God provides many of the creations as sources of food for us and the animals. All have a part in what God created, whether scientists want to believe it or not.

If the theory of evolution was not so widespread and accepted by so many, one could think that all we know about existing emanating from some kind of a single cell something is just plain silly. Look at all of the different kinds of spiders in the world alone. Then there are the numerous kinds of birds, both those who can fly and those who cannot. So many different kinds of fish and species of each fish exist; some live in fresh water and others in salt water.

But, I want to zoom in on one of the hardest working creations of God known to man, and that is our little friend the ant. As with many other animals, fish, and insects, the ant has numerous different species. They range from the little pest who always seems to find his way into our homes, to the red ants of the Southwest known as "fire ants," to the ferocious soldier ants better known as army ants. Again, all are creations of God.

Although I have never seen an army ant up close, I am told (and the information on the internet supports it) that these rather large-sized ants are land piranhas. One does not want to be caught by a platoon of these bad boys, or the only thing that others will find left of you are your bones.

Then there are the detested (personal reference) fire ants that are found all over the southern USA, as well as other places on earth. As a boy growing up in Texas, I had more than one occasion to find out just why they are called fire ants and the pain they can inflict on a pair of bare feet.

Then we come to the little pesty ant that we find so often marching a trail from the nest to the food source they found inside or outside of our homes and back to the nest or ant mound. These little members of the insect world can be found just about everywhere, doing whatever is needed to maintain their colony, each with their own job.

Ordinarily, this would be a rather boring point, when defending the fact of creation, and the myth of evolution. But, this little insect is quite a hard-working sort.

Despite my bad interactions with fire ants, as a boy in Texas, I would often watch a trail of ants as they went about their chores. On many occasions, I would see some of these workers carrying something like a piece of a leaf that was at least three times their size, headed for the colony entrance. The little creatures would lift up their center legs and hold the leaf in place,

Creation A to Z

and move it from where it was obtained, across the rather lengthy distance of the trail, to the entrance of the ant mound.

Upon arrival at the entrance, other workers would set about reducing the leaf into a size that would allow it to be taken inside the colony. This almost orchestrated process of maintaining the colony was just fascinating to this young boy. Little did I know just how much of a lesson God was teaching me.

Some of these ant species are so small that a newborn baby's foot could probably crush ten of them at one time. Also, no matter how much we try and apply insecticide to kill them, these resilient members of the insect family just keep coming back into our lives—another fact of God's intervention in all things that He created.

I live near the big city of Baltimore, Maryland. At the city's center is the harbor that leads into the Chesapeake Bay. In this area, known as Inner Harbor, is a very large aquarium. I have visited this aquarium on many occasions, viewing special exhibits like the jellyfish, beluga whales, and stingrays. In the center is a very large tank of ocean life, including some small sharks. On one visit, I watched as a shark had itself a meal by eating one of the other fish in the tank. Strange as it may be, here again is evidence of God's provision of food for one of His creations.

In the grasslands of Africa, God has provided some animals as food for other animals. The meat-eating lions and cheetahs will hunt for food animals like the wildebeest, gazelles, and impalas. Baboons will eat berries and termites. The giraffe will eat leaves from trees that only it can reach, and the mighty elephant will devour tons of food each day.

This chapter could easily turn into a documentary from National Geographic, listing all of the creatures God has created, and how He provides for every one of them. The many va-

Creation Is a Science

rieties of animals are matched by the many varieties of food sources. The diversity of creatures is amazing, yet many are found in only one place on earth, although others are found just about everywhere. Even some creatures from the ocean are found in only one place, while others swim the oceans worldwide.

These creatures, like my friends the ants, come in many sizes. In the oceans, you will find one of the main sources of food to many fish is that of plankton, tiny sea life that may or may not develop into a fish. This miniature food source is devoured by the tons per day by very large creatures of the deep like the manta ray and whale shark.

Do you understand where I am going in this chapter? I am not trying to provide you with a Zoology or Oceanography lesson. Instead, I am showing you just how diverse are the creatures we have on this earth. Again, all are created by God for a purpose, yet the scientists would have us believe that everything came from that single cell something. As I said, if it were not for these folks doing all they can to shove this down the throats of our school students, this would be a rather humorous statement.

Go ahead and ask yourself, just how gullible do these scientists think we are? How can we believe that all came from a Big Bang, a particular chemical reaction that formed a single cell something, and as the millions of years went by developed into the living creatures on earth, including humans? It all comes back to the same issue here, they just cannot accept that God commanded everything to be created in six days, and it was so.

16

Teaching the Truth

I have a very bad habit, since the coming of social media, to tear into a subject that is detrimental to anything Christian. Just like my mentor and favorite Bible character, the Apostle Peter, I will set my hooks and jump into the subject full bore.

Now before you criticize me for not showing the love of Christ, I will tell you that my comments are kind with a bit of weight behind them. You will not get anywhere today going off on a person or problem, in the same manner a bear goes into a river or stream after a fish. By doing this, you just turned off that person to whom you are responding, or those causing the problem, and you will be only talking to yourself.

In addressing the issue of teaching only evolution in our schools and removing any mention of God's creation, we must handle the problem with the love of Christ but with the weight of an anvil to back you up. This is where all of that planning, research, and intelligence I wrote about earlier come together.

One of the most frustrating problems we as Christians face today comes from us opposing actions like denying the teaching of creation in our schools. We are immediately labeled as Bible thumpers, bigots, narrow-minded, biased, and some other references that I would not say to anyone. It seems that if Christians want something, it just has to be wrong for everybody. When we get these kinds of responses that can be very harsh in the language utilized, we must stay calm since we are God's representatives in the matter.

I have been in a situation where you just want to cut loose on the opposition and give them a new way of thinking. This is when we must keep our cool, take a walk, talk to God about how we feel, and turn down the blood pressure. Although we do not like it, Satan and his demons are very much alive and well in our society today. Anything they can do to get under our skin, irritate our feelings, and destroy our testimony for God is their goal. When they are successful, God's people miss the mark and fail in their purpose and desire for change.

The old saying, which is as accurate today as it was years ago, really fits into this discussion. It states: "The squeaking wheel gets the oil." We must accept that we will face setbacks, lose a battle here and there, and realize that our opposition is convinced that all things Christian are wrong. But God expects us to keep fighting for what is right. We need to stay the course to demand our schools teach the truth and not total fabrications like that of evolution only.

Also, we must avoid nagging, being pests, and just plain turning off those whom we want to change. If you are anything like me, I can be quite confrontational; however, sometimes we need to get out the honey instead of the howitzers.

It is not just the teaching of evolution in our schools we must stand up against. Our students today are being bombed with other adverse actions, opinions, and in plain English, sins of the world. The liberal community's far left-leaning Social Progressives (SPs) and others who are under that Satanic influence are now insisting on adding the Lesbian, Gay, Bisexual, and Transgender (LGBTQ) movement's lifestyle into the schools.

Some schools across our nation teach kids the pluses and minuses of being gay and in some extremes are even introducing gender-neutral restrooms into the schools. The schools are sup-

Teaching the Truth

posed to be concerned about the health of our students, yet they allow this unhealthy, abnormal, immoral, unnatural, and (in my opinion) mentally challenged lifestyle into the schools.

They argue that people are born gay, so we must accept it and provide for the person's needs. This opinion is just as baseless as the teaching of evolution. Being gay is a choice, and sin is totally responsible for its existence in a person.

Our Christian students face this problem and not just in school. These issues, difficulties, and challenges are everywhere in our world today, and that is because Satan and his demons are working overtime to keep as many as they can from knowing about God and His Son Jesus Christ.

Today, those who demand our schools and employers provide and bring forth only the truth in all things, are labeled as naysayers, disrupters, and many other references. The simple act of just doing what is right, telling and teaching the truth, and doing what is good for our fellow man and woman is also honoring God.

We, as servants of God, just cannot sit back and hope that all will come out right in the end. Satan does not want it to come out right, so unless we intervene and get into the weeds of the problems and issues at hand, he wins the battle, and we and our students lose.

Ignoring the problem will not make it go away either, because Satan is going after every part of our lives to interfere with our service to and for God. The enemy wants us to fail, and that is just exactly why we must stay in contact with our God through prayer, devotions private and corporately, being involved in church activities, and above all making our feelings quite clear at the voting booth. Demand the truth be taught or make a change.

Conclusion

No Is Unacceptable

References: *Wex Legal Dictionary*, Establishment and Free Exercise Clauses to the 1st Amendment to the U.S. Constitution. Pennsylvania Constitution, Article I, Section 3.

The judgment of the U.S. District Court for Middle Pennsylvania dated December 20, 2005 mentioned the two references I have listed for this chapter, as supporting the ruling denying the including of Intelligent Design in that school district near my home; ruling that creationism "is not a science."

Now I am no lawyer, but I can listen to plain English, and I feel these references support the teaching to be inclusive more than they ever support the denial. First, the Establishment Clause to the 1st Amendment of the U.S. Constitution states that Congress "shall make no law, respecting the establishment of religion." Further, it declares that government cannot condone or reject a religion.

The Pennsylvania Constitution reference states, "All men have a natural and indefeasible right to worship Almighty God, according to the dictates of their own consciences." Also, even the Preamble to the Pennsylvania Constitution acknowledges the existence of Almighty God.

It is my opinion that this judge must have used the reasoning from Common Core in his 139-page decision from these two sources of law that there was a legal precedent to deny teaching Intelligent Design. From the Establishment Clause, the decision whether Intelligent Design is or is not taught was not to be determined by any branch of government.

Then you have the Pennsylvania Constitution that in both the document's Preamble, as well as in Article I, Section 3 gives man the freedom to worship Almighty God according to his or her conscience.

Okay, we have successfully (in my opinion), debunked the judgment of this Federal Court. However, this does not change the decision of the local school board to eliminate any teaching or mention of Intelligent Design in the school district. Here is where the voters within that district must utilize their vote the next time these liberal opponents of creation come up for re-election. Want Intelligent Design taught in that district? Vote to boot them out of the board!

In the USA today, the courts are making law from the bench, despite the Constitution prohibiting them. This Federal Court judge, in Harrisburg, Pennsylvania, listened to the arguments of this case, incorrectly interpreted the law, and told the school district no. Well, no is just not acceptable when the law supports Intelligent Design being included in a school's curriculum.

On the local level, some house cleaning is needing to be done by the district voters. Get some people who are willing to serve on the board, support including Intelligent Design in the school, vote them in, and boot out those who oppose it. Although the courts are trying to overturn the votes of the people, the majority still rules the day in the USA.

I have referred to the issue in this school district near my home, but this situation can exist almost anywhere in our country and on almost any anti-Christian issue. Further, in all of my research, and even in attempting to make contact with the district or someone living in that district, I was unable to verify if this situation still exists or has since been corrected in that school district. I pray that it has, because denying students the right they have to hear all sides is denying them their basic right to a complete and full education.

Our courts have made numerous decisions in the past, where the ruling of no is just not acceptable. Most notably are three decisions by SCOTUS, where we the citizens were told no without any Constitutional support. We were told no to prayer and Bible reading in the schools in 1963, we were told no to bans on abortion in 1973, and most recently we were told no to bans on same-sex marriages in 2015.

As I have stated previously in this book, these no judgments did not stop with these decisions. You have organizations and groups like the American Civil Liberties Union (ACLU) (that I call the Anti-Christ Legal Underwriters), the Foundation for Religious Freedom (FFRF), the Americans United for the Separation of Church and State (AU), and the Military Religious Freedom Foundation (MRFF) doing all they can by threatening suits to force the removal of Christian crosses, the Ten Commandments, nativity scenes, and anything else associated with Christianity.

This book may have zeroed in on *Creation Is a Science*; however, we face so many other threats, attacks, and suits to deny us our freedom to worship Almighty God. All of these actions come back around to the influence of Satan and his demons on our world today.

People just do not understand how we Christians can express love for sinners, yet we, like our God, hate the sin. How can God be such a loving God yet let disasters occur? Why can't a gay or lesbian person live that lifestyle and be a Christian too? Who is God, if He actually exists, to tell me how I must live my life and to what standards? All of these kinds of questions, and many others, are fired at us every day.

Explaining that we believe and follow God, the instructions in His Word the Bible, and the need to accept Jesus Christ as one's Savior to guarantee our eternal home in heaven by faith are just not understood by those who are blinded by sin.

Another question that I have had asked is, "Just exactly where is your God?" This is an old question but is just as valid to the sinners today. In the very beginning of the space race between the USSR and the USA, the Soviets first man to orbit the earth, Yuri Gagarin, was quoted upon his return to earth that "There is no God because I could not see him up there."

The truth is that what he saw in space, and what we see, feel, eat, and breathe here on earth is all evidence of God. Only through the actions of a Supreme Being we call God could our earth be formed as it is, land and water created, and everything from the little ant to the mighty elephant walk the same earth.

Before we close, let's look at one more piece of evidence of God's creation and just how perfect it is. Going back to the Big Bang theory, no matter which theory the evolutionists hold to, claim that from that explosion, all of the planets, comets, stars, and the sun were formed. The debate is currently on whether what was previously called a planet named Pluto is actually a planet. When I was in school, and most hold to this, we were taught that nine planets make up our particular solar system.

Although Mercury is about thirty-six million miles from the sun, NASA tells us that temperatures on Mercury cannot support life. Venus is wrapped in poisonous fog-like gases and also cannot support life. Looking out at Mars and the remaining planets and their respective moons, although scientists keep trying to prove life exists elsewhere, none of them can support life in many ways.

Creation Is a Science

It is only here on earth that many forms of life can survive and flourish. Only here on earth do we have the two types of atmosphere that allow one type of God's creation to provide for another type of God's creation and help the first type of God's creation. Only on earth do we have the exact and correct temperatures to allow for life to exist, breathe, eat, and populate the planet. Yes, only on earth can this fact be true because God made it that way.

Shortly after man began to fly, we learned that the temperatures just a few thousand feet above were much colder than on the surface of the earth. The men who fought in the air war of World War II had to wear electric jackets to keep warm because at about twenty-five thousand feet, the temperatures could be over minus forty degrees. But how can it be colder the higher and closer you get to the sun? Here is just another miracle of God's perfect creation for all the creatures and we humans who live on this place we call earth.

Several layers of atmospheric filters make up our planet's ability to support life, filtering out certain destructive rays and meteors, while at the same time retaining the heat from the sun to keep us warm within life standards.

These are facts that science has proven to exist, like the famous Van Allen belts, etc. It is also a fact proven by the same scientists that nowhere else does this type of atmospheric arrangement exist. Really, yet we all came from that same Big Bang? Well, here is where no certainly does apply. Fact: God created all that we know to exist, PERIOD!

A Final Thought

We have only touched a few of the examples, evidence, and just plain proof that evolution is nothing but a very bad and baseless theory. I could haul in so many other types of sea life, land animals, etc. No matter how much you try to overwhelm these scientists, they are just not going to accept the existence of God, the fact that He created all that is, and that He did it in six days by just speaking it into existence. Because of this unacceptable attitude, we should wonder what we can do to change how this affects our schools and society in general.

Something that we cannot change is that from time to time Satan and his demons are going to win a battle, just like the baseless court and school board rulings. This is where I must urge all of you not to take an "oh well" attitude and just throw up your hands in frustration. If we do this, Satan has won the battle, but if we keep plugging away, keep visiting that voting booth, and most of all, keep the word of mouth line active, he may have won for now, but in the end, he will lose.

During the Pacific portion of World War II, Japan was confident that their attack on Pearl Harbor would prevent anyone from stopping their expansionist invasions. However, the allies started on a very slow, yet determined plan of island hopping until Japan finally surrendered. Yes, the road was filled with many of our boys and girls coming back in boxes, but in the end, we celebrated the victory.

The same plan can be applied here, no matter the issue. What is wrong for our schools, our cities, our nation, and just wrong period is just that—wrong. So break out the multiple waves of attack against this movement and pursue to the end to right the wrong. Get the media involved, write letters to the elected officials and the newspaper editors, spread the word to area churches, and on the list can go on.

In today's world, it seems the minority or single person gets their way over the will of the majority. Here is where that visit to the voting booth, attending town halls, and participating in the election process yourself can and will make a change. Keep praying, talking, screaming (where necessary), attending those board meetings, etc. to make sure those who make these wrong decisions are very well aware that you want it changed. Hang tough, but keep those anvils in your back pockets.

These actions do not need to stop with the curriculum either. A recent news item described that a family in Maryland found out that their daughter had been required to commit allegiance to Allah as part of a school history class studying the Middle East religions. The family, devout Christians, filed a suit against the school district for requiring their daughter to do this, contrary to their belief in God.

This type of instruction in our schools should not be tolerated either. Yes, Allah is the Arabic word for god; however, Islam does not worship the God of creation. Instead, Allah is just Satan by another name, and that is why I wrote that Allah means god (little 'g') in Arabic.

Our youth are being attacked on all sides by Satan, in his desperate desire to keep them from knowing God, and the salvation that comes from accepting Jesus Christ as their Savior. I urge you not just to turn a deaf ear, and a blind eye to those things going on around you today. Sometimes just exposing these things will cause them to be withdrawn and disappear.

However, you and others with you just might have to take on the board, the administration, or even elected political officials and face them with the issue at hand. If they do not listen, remove them and do it yourself!

A Final Thought

An example of how prayer and being involved can change things comes from an issue I described in some of my earlier books. A person, identified as an atheist, saw three crosses that stood alongside a road just south of the town of Dillsburg, Pennsylvania, on U.S. Route 15 southbound and filed a suit to have them removed. In the original court proceedings, the judge ordered them removed, and the violation of the mythical separation of church and state was referenced as the basis for the ruling.

Recently, while discussing my books, this issue was raised. I was informed that those crosses still stand alongside that road because the court's decision had been appealed, and the lower court's decision was overturned. Praise the Lord, as those crosses that had stood in the same position for quite some time would continue to stand and not be removed.

The same thing can happen with the Federal Court decision I referenced at the beginning of this book. The court stated that "creationism is not a science"; and because of this view, it cannot be taught in the public schools. If applied as the court ruled, this could remove the teaching of Intelligent Design from all public schools in the USA.

This decision is invalid, as there are several facilities worldwide that research God's creation of all things as a science, for example, the Institute for Creation Research (see www.icr.org) in Dallas, Texas, and the Discovery Institute (see www.discovery.org) in Seattle, Washington.

In addition, reader, you and your family may want to take a vacation to the Creation Museum in Petersburg, Kentucky, and the Ark Encounter in Williamstown, Kentucky, into your bucket list. Both of these very instructional and science-based Christian attractions are located across the Ohio River about an hour from Cincinnati, Ohio. Here you will find numerous exhibits demonstrating the science behind both events in the Bible (see www.answersingenesis.org).

Prayer, following God's will, and obeying His desires for our lives can change things despite the actions of Satan and his demonic followers. As I have written before, every time I hear the sounds of a thunderstorm, I am reminded that God is still in control of all things. The weather service employees cannot stop the storms from coming, nor can Satan and his demons take away what God decides will remain in place, or they will be corrected. Put your trust in God and just watch Him work in whatever your needs are or the problems you face in our world.

God bless America!

References

Many of the references I listed in this book are readily available on the internet, at your local courthouse, or by contacting your Congressional or Senatorial representative's offices. Maybe your particular issue was not addressed in this book. Just search the internet on your issue's name, and you will probably find more information available to you than you thought could exist.

For more information on our Christian faith and how to stand firm on God's Word, contact:

• The Billy Graham Evangelistic Association at www.bgea.org.
• In Touch Ministries of Dr. Charles Stanley at www.intouch.org.
• Turning Point, Dr. David Jeremiah at www.davidjeremiah.org.
• Leading the Way, Dr. Michael Youssef at www.ltw.org.

Sources of free legal representation are available from the following:
• Alliance Defending Freedom (ADF), www.adflegal.org.
• American Center for Law and Justice (ACLJ), https://aclj.org.

About the Author

Kevin Turnbaugh was born on August 10, 1954, and graduated from Hanover High School in 1972. He was employed for a short time in the meat packing industry, then for 13 years in the shoe industry. For the next 27 years and 8 months, he served as a civilian employee of the Army. In 1999, he went blind from the eye disease Retinitis Pigmentosa. He is the author of four previous books, and his website is: www.timewitnessing.com.

www.ingramcontent.com/pod-product-compliance
Lightning Source LLC
Chambersburg PA
CBHW052111110526
44592CB00013B/1559